"Margaret Paul is one of our high priestesses, always taking us deeper into the mysteries of our own hearts and casting light on all she sees there."

—**Marianne Williamson**, #1 *New York Times* bestselling author of
A Return to Love

"Margaret Paul has always been on the leading edge of the transformation and healing movement, and ahead of her time in how to support responsibility taking, empowerment, a sense of wholeness, and connection within and without. Her commitment to supporting people in their healing journeys has had her share her wisdom, information, and processes with great clarity and certainty.

Tending to the ruptures in our sense of connection with our selves and spirit and in our relationships, Margaret Paul's invitation to us through this book is nothing short of revelatory, empowering, relieving, and deeply kind.

Inner Bonding has been a staple in my own personal journey home to wholeness. The effects of Margaret's teachings have touched my soul and life in a way that will see me grateful to her for the rest of my life."

—**Alanis Morissette**, artist, activist, and teacher

"There is nothing more important than self-love, and *The Inner Bonding Workbook* is the ultimate self-love guide. Margaret Paul is the master of showing people how to truly, madly, deeply fall in love with themselves in a way that is authentic and lasting. This work will help you move through any limitations and self-doubts, and make the way for a life ahead that's filled with the light and love of your soul. Divine grace is in action in these pages."

—**Marci Shimoff**, #1 *New York Times* bestselling author of *Happy for
No Reason*, and coauthor of *Chicken Soup for the Woman's Soul*

"*The Inner Bonding Workbook* is a beautiful invitation to attend to our physical, emotional, and mental health. Margaret Paul's writing is so filled with grace, I felt like she was tending to me personally. She creates such a field of safety that before I knew it, I was deep in my inner landscape facing some of my core wounds. *The Inner Bonding Workbook* provides a brilliant road map for anyone wanting to explore their spiritual identity and let go of the bonds that anchor us to our past."

—**Sandra Ingerman, MA**, award-winning author of twelve books, including
Walking in Light and *The Book of Ceremony*

"Here in this book is a powerful process for self-healing inner pain, addictions, and relationship problems. *The Inner Bonding Workbook* takes you step by step through healing the deep, and often unconscious, false beliefs that may be keeping you limited in your physical and emotional health, and in your ability to connect with a higher source of love, comfort, and wisdom. You will find yourself changed in profoundly positive ways as you work through this workbook. A must-read for anyone ready to step into living their joyful life!"

> —**Sue Morter**, founder of Morter Institute for BioEnergetics, master of bioenergetic medicine, quantum field visionary, and author of *The Energy Codes*

"To me, learning to acknowledge our feelings and finding healthy, loving ways to address them is the most wonderful gift we can give ourselves. Margaret Paul's body of work is one of the best at taking us on that journey. *The Inner Bonding Workbook* really lights up the way."

> —**Lindsay Wagner**, actor and human potential advocate

"Inner Bonding is a much-needed tool for today's current state of stress and chaos. It gives you a sense of peace and support no one can ever take away. Thank you, Margaret!"

> —**Lisa Garr**, host of *The Aware Show*, and author of *Becoming Aware*

"In order to hear that still, small voice of inner wisdom guiding us into ever-unfolding truth and joy, we must learn to love ourselves. *The Inner Bonding Workbook* takes us by the hand and shows us how. Margaret Paul is the wise, nurturing voice of love that we all need to hear, to let go of the noise of the past and live into a graceful new way of being."

> —**Miranda Macpherson**, author of *The Way of Grace*

"I'm in love with this book. Inner Bonding is my go-to resource for everyone who wants to learn the deepest lessons of self-love. *The Inner Bonding Workbook* is now my favorite Inner Bonding resource. This workbook makes the reader feel like a live participant in a masterfully executed workshop. The exercises, explanations, and stories guide you with compassion and breathtaking clarity through every step of this life-changing process. This is the book I've been waiting for. If you're looking for healing, joy, and peace, *The Inner Bonding Workbook* is one of the greatest gifts you can give yourself."

> —**Ken Page**, LCSW, psychotherapist, author of *Deeper Dating*, and host of *The Deeper Dating Podcast*

"Spiritual soul food! Discover the power of learning to access, at any moment, the incredible wisdom, peace, joy, and unending source of Divine energy. In *The Inner Bonding Workbook*, Margaret Paul shares the six life-enhancing steps to loving and healing yourself, accessing your Divine guidance moment by moment, and learning to joyfully manifest your passion and purpose. A must-read for those ready to release the shackles and stories of the past."

> —**Linda Joy**, best-selling publisher, visibility catalyst for visionary female messengers, and publisher of *Aspire Magazine*

"Margaret Paul is an expert at helping you clear debilitating energy-and-consciousness 'contractions'—like negative beliefs and stuck emotion—as well as the distracting clutter caused by a jumpy mind, looking outside for answers, or identifying yourself as only physical and mental. She makes it easy to identify yourself as your unlimited soul, instead of as one of the walking wounded. This wonderful workbook synthesizes years of her experience guiding thousands of people to release unnecessary suffering and find wisdom and joy as their true self. It's invaluable!"

> —**Penney Peirce**, respected visionary, expert on intuition and personal transformation, and author of ten books, including *Frequency*, *Leap of Perception*, and *Transparency*

The

INNER
BONDING
Workbook

Six Steps *to* Healing Yourself *and* Connecting with Your Divine Guidance

MARGARET PAUL, PhD

REVEAL PRESS
AN IMPRINT OF NEW HARBINGER PUBLICATIONS

Publisher's Note

This publication is designed to provide accurate and authoritative information in regard to the subject matter covered. It is sold with the understanding that the publisher is not engaged in rendering psychological, financial, legal, or other professional services. If expert assistance or counseling is needed, the services of a competent professional should be sought.

Distributed in Canada by Raincoast Books

Copyright © 2019 by Margaret Paul
          New Harbinger Publications, Inc.
          5674 Shattuck Avenue
          Oakland, CA 94609
          www.newharbinger.com

Lines from "On the First Day" from RUMI by Rumi, translated by Jonathan Star, copyright © 1997 by Jonathan Star. Used by permission of Tarcher, an imprint of Penguin Publishing Group, a division of Penguin Random House LLC. All rights reserved.

Cover design by Amy Shoup

Acquired by Jennye Garibaldi

Edited by Jennifer Eastman

All Rights Reserved

Library of Congress Cataloging-in-Publication Data on file

Printed in the United States of America

22   21   20

10   9   8   7   6   5   4   3

This book is dedicated to my Divine guidance, who lovingly dictated this book to me, bringing me great joy in the process of writing. It is deeply fulfilling for me to receive the wisdom of my Divine guidance and share it with others. I feel blessed by her Divine presence.

Contents

Foreword

There are two faces to all spiritual traditions. The first of course is religion, which offers rules and regulations that all good followers must do their best to adhere to. Yet the second is mysticism. That which initiates us into the deeper, more enchanted and magical dimensions of life through the cultivation of a direct connection with the Divine. The poet Rumi described it this way:

> I looked upon every Cross, in every church,
> yet He was not there.
>
> . . . .
>
> Then I looked within my own heart
> and there I found Him—
> He was nowhere else.

While poets, saints and sages have written about this sacred and deeply personal dance with the Divine for millennia, mysticism only became available to regular folks like us in 1938, when philosopher Ralph Waldo Emerson stood before the graduating class of Harvard Divinity School to boldly declare that Jesus was simply an example of what's possible for us all when we open ourselves to cultivate a direct relationship with the Divine. It became a huge scandal and he was quickly renounced as an atheist. He was not invited back to Harvard again for another thirty years.

Margaret Paul is such a rebel, sticking her neck out from the safety of her psychological credentials to again share the good news that we are by nature connected to a force and field of Life greater than us that is designed to guide us in the direction of our greatest good. By sharing her step-by-step process of how we can connect with our own deeper knowing to find our way home to wholeness, and then allow our knowing to guide our growth journey, Dr. Paul defies traditional psychology and opens a portal that promises to shave years off our time sitting on the couch trying to sort through the rubble of the past.

As Emerson did in his day, Dr. Paul now encourages us to begin relating to God as our partner in life, rather than as a glorified and somewhat scary parent-in-the-sky. She inspires us to grow our ability to be modern day mystics who are fully capable of hearing the voice of truth, wisdom, healing and love within ourselves, whenever we go within to listen.

I must admit I'm relieved. For all these years, we have blindly followed the psychological prescriptions of those educated in the ways of the psyche, as if they knew better than we ourselves did how we could get well and heal. Though my psychotherapists were all deeply well-meaning and had years of education under their belts, never once in my years of personal therapy did any of them suggest I close my eyes to connect with my own inner guidance to help me solve some of my most pressing problems. Nor was I ever taught, in my many years of graduate training while I studied to become a licensed therapist myself, that I should do this with any of my clients.

So, the brave Margaret Paul is also the brilliant Margaret Paul. For I now know firsthand that she's right in what she's saying. That until we have this awakening to the wisdom within, we will chase our own tales by endlessly analyzing the past rather than knowingly navigating our way to wellbeing and wholeness in the present. Having had the privilege of teaching tens of thousands of people over the past twenty years, I can attest that this capacity to turn within to find and follow our own intuitive guidance is one of the most important keys to being liberated to create happy, healthy lives that are no longer weighed down or defined by the traumas of the past.

The other piece Dr. Paul so beautifully teaches in this treasure of a book is how we can cultivate a relationship with our own inner child. Like the rings printed inside the trunk of a tree, we carry each stage of our lives deep within. And when a wound remains unresolved, that particular ring in our psyche can cause us to unconsciously behave in ways that re-wound us time and time again. By following Dr. Paul's protocol, we can finally put to rest the hurts of the past and be free to live rich, full lives, keeping only the compassion and wisdom gained and releasing the rest.

All this is to say, you are in good hands with my friend, Dr. Margaret Paul. Having picked up this book, you are now in for the healing ride of your life. Savor the wisdom she offers. For truly, it will awaken you to the pathway of inner peace and unleash a new sense of purpose and delight in your life.

—Katherine Woodward Thomas
    New York Times bestselling author of
    Calling in "The One" and *Conscious Uncoupling*

Introduction

The Joy of At-Will Divine Connection

All of us would love to know for certain that we are on this planet for some purpose. That we are not here simply to suffer—to feel empty and alone, anxious, or depressed—but rather to joyfully go through life with inner peace and creatively manifest our passion and purpose.

What would you give to *know* that

- you are here for a reason,

- you are never alone,

- you are always being guided in your highest good,

- you can learn to access this guidance moment by moment, and

- your connection will give you the ability to joyfully manifest your passion and purpose?

As a young woman, I would have given anything to know that these were even possibilities for me. I was stuck with false beliefs that I had absorbed growing up: beliefs about who we are, about what we can and can't control, about what life here is really about, and about what the Divine is or is not. This kept me feeling limited and stuck, suffering from anxiety, depression, emptiness, and aloneness. I was disconnected from myself, from my feelings, and from the love and wisdom of spiritual guidance.

While some people feel disconnected because they are taught that God is a judgmental man in the sky who is always watching them and that they will be punished in hell for their sins, I wasn't raised in a religious household. I wasn't taught that there was anything higher than my own limited mind. My parents were atheists to whom the idea of God was anathema. I often heard my father say, with a very judgmental tone, "Anyone who believes in God is just using that as a crutch." Yet even from my youngest days, I had a deep sense that I was not my body and that there was a source of knowing available to me, but I had no idea how to access it. I had no support for developing my spiritual nature.

I suffered from rather severe anxiety. When I was five, my rageful, narcissistic mother, believing that my anxiety was my fault, brought me to a psychiatrist. After speaking with each of us, he told me to tell my mother to stop yelling at me. I clearly remember thinking, *You tell her. I'm only five, and she doesn't listen to me.* My next thought was, *I can do a better job than you*, and that's when I decided I wanted to be a psychologist!

I was a sensitive, empathic, and compassionate child, and it took me many years to understand that neither of my parents was remotely capable of any sensitivity, empathy, or compassion. They were often in pain, and being sensitive to others' feelings, I learned to absorb their pain and do everything I could to take it away. I became addicted to taking care of them, and because they would be angry if I was in pain, I learned to completely ignore my own feelings.

By the time I was in my late teens, I was miserable. I had a strong sense that there was something missing in my life, but I had no idea what it was. There had to be more to life than the constant anxiety, aloneness, and insecurity I felt. I went into psychoanalysis for four and a half years, four days a week. I learned everything about my past and why I felt miserable, but not what to do about it. My analyst dismissed me when I was twenty-three, saying, "You're analyzed." Believing that this meant I was healthy, and believing that getting married and having children would bring me the peace, security, and self-worth I wanted, I got married. When this didn't bring me the relief I sought, I tried many different therapists and different kinds of therapies to heal my anxiety. None of them worked for me.

After my third child was born, I started to have brief experiences of something that lifted my anxiety, something that felt oddly familiar. That's when I remembered that, as a young child, I had a deep knowing that I was not my body and that there was something more to life than what it presented on the surface.

That's when I started on my spiritual search—a search to connect with a source of spiritual love, comfort, and wisdom. I had read enough about spirituality to know that this was likely a path I needed to learn more about. I acquired a guru and joined a meditation group. Again, I had momentary experiences of inner peace and joy from what I now knew was a spiritual connection, but I had no idea how to have this experience whenever I wanted it. It felt like it would just happen to me, like I didn't have any say about it. And fleeting connection wasn't enough for me. In fact, each time I felt it, I wasn't really sure it had happened. Was I just making it up, because I wanted it so much?

I wanted to be able to *choose* this experience, and I wanted to know for sure that I'm never alone—that spiritual help is *always* here for me. But how to know it? How to feel it? How to access it? Momentary experiences of Spirit didn't resolve my anxiety and feeling of being so alone, so I was deeply motivated to learn how to do this.

At-Will Connection

I spent many years trying to achieve *at-will* Divine connection. For me, *at will* means that I can have this connection anytime I want it, even all the time, if that's what I want. I didn't want to feel that Spirit was choosing me at random and that I just had to wait for this loving energy to come to me. I wanted to discover how to access this incredible wisdom, peace, joy, and unending source of energy at any moment.

I became a psychotherapist, but after practicing traditional psychotherapy for seventeen years, I wasn't happy with the results. Through all the different forms of therapy I'd had, through my spiritual search and work with clients, I had come to know that no true healing occurs without a spiritual connection. But I still didn't know how to have this at will or how to help my clients have this. It was at that time that I started to pray for a teacher to come into my life who understood spiritual connection, and that's when I met Dr. Erika Chopich, who later became the co-creator of Inner Bonding with me—and my best friend. Erika had half of what would be the Inner Bonding process, and I had the other half, so of course we had to meet! Soon after we met, Spirit guided us to creating the Inner Bonding process, which has now been evolving for thirty-four years.

The Insights of Inner Bonding

For me and many of my clients, our unique gifts and deeper sense of purpose were buried under fears and false beliefs that we developed as we were growing up. We lost contact with the individual blueprint we each have regarding how to joyfully express our purpose on the planet. Perhaps you feel the same way. Because of my disconnection, I had to relearn that my purpose on the planet is to evolve in my ability to love and to creatively manifest the gifts I have been given. I did this by connecting with my inner and higher guidance. As I did, I also discovered that this is the purpose for all of us.

Through the Inner Bonding process, you can regain this deeper knowing and become able to creatively express your unique gifts. Finding inner peace, safety, and self-worth comes from an internal shift in beliefs and in how we treat ourselves—rather than from external validation. When we have no way to heal the beliefs that limit us and cut us off from our Divine guidance, the peace and joy of life elude us. It's these false beliefs that then fuel our self-rejecting and self-abandoning behaviors, which are the underlying causes of our suffering. I know from personal experience what it's like to live disconnected from myself and my spiritual guidance, as well as what it's like to live with it. For me, this has been the difference between suffering and joy.

There is no one "right" form of Divine guidance. We have many names for our spiritual source of love and wisdom: God, Goddess, Spirit, higher power, the Lord, beloved, Jehovah, Yahweh, Holy Spirit, nature, the light, the source, universal intelligence, universal life force, the all, the creator, Jesus, Buddha, Allah, guardian angel, and inner or outer wise-self or higher-self. So use the words that work for you and connect through a form that resonates.

A High "Frequency" Is Essential for At-Will Divine Connection

Divine connection has to do with "frequency," and it was with Erika's help that I discovered how to attain the frequency I needed for at-will Divine connection. I had discovered through reading, taking courses, and meeting some people who were key to my spiritual search that I needed to develop a high frequency—a high level of vibrancy—to connect to Spirit. However, until I met Erika, I had no idea what it meant to have a high frequency or how to achieve this in an ongoing way.

Our frequency is the rate at which our energy vibrates. Energy is the level of lightness and vitality we experience. For example, if you walk into a room full of closed, angry, rejecting, and blaming people, you might feel like you want to leave because of the heavy, dark energy in the room. If you stay, you might end up feeling anxious or depressed. That's a low frequency. But if you walk into a room of open and caring people, you will likely feel welcomed and relaxed due to the light, vibrant energy in the room. That's a high frequency.

Another way of understanding frequency is by thinking about television or radio stations. Each station has a different frequency, which is what enables you to tune in to what you want. When you want to tune in to a television station, you turn to a particular channel, which has a particular frequency. Just because you can't see the television or radio waves doesn't mean they aren't there. You accept their presence because the program you want comes on the television or radio. Just as you turn to a particular radio station or television channel to connect with what you want to hear or see, you can learn to turn to a particular inner frequency to connect with your personal source of Divine guidance. And just as you don't have to *believe* that the radio and television waves are there, because you experience the result of tuning in to your station, you don't have to believe that your Divine guidance is here for you. *You will know it is true when you experience it, and the exercises in this book will enable you to do that.*

One of the reasons most of us can't see Spirit is because the energy of Spirit moves very fast, which means that Spirit exists at a higher frequency than we do. Because we are in bodies, our frequency is slower and more earthbound than that of Spirit. Imagine if our energy were moving as fast as the propeller of a plane or a hummingbird's wings. We would have a hard time seeing each other! However, we *can* learn to raise our frequency high enough to connect with Spirit.

Divine connection occurs when we are energetically available to the higher frequency of our Divine guidance. Since we have free will, we get to choose, moment by moment, whether we want to be open or closed, welcoming or rejecting, and this choice is one of the two major aspects of what affects our frequency.

It was when I finally discovered the two secrets for raising my frequency high enough that I found I could consistently experience at-will Divine connection. This discovery dramatically changed my life; it gave me the ability to access the wisdom, creativity, and support of Spirit to manifest my dreams.

I'm excited to share these secrets with you. The first secret I discovered is that our frequency is greatly determined by the *food we eat*, and the second secret is that our frequency is also greatly determined by our *thoughts and resulting actions*.

Junk Foods and Junk Thoughts

Junk foods and junk thoughts lower our frequency to the point of spiritual disconnection. Many highly processed and packaged foods contain high levels of devitalized ingredients and additives—such as sugar, high fructose corn syrup, genetically modified organisms (GMOs), altered fats, preservatives, and colorings—as well as the residues of factory farming, such as antibiotics and pesticides. The low frequency of these ingredients greatly affects your frequency level, which makes it much harder to connect with your Divine guidance. (For more information about the foods that lower frequency, see my book *Diet for Divine Connection*.)

The fact that these foods are created to taste good makes it challenging to avoid them. But how do you feel after eating a cheeseburger, a bag of French fries, and a large soft drink? If you were tuned in to your feelings, you might notice feeling lethargic or depressed. Is the fleeting taste of these foods really worth getting sick or feeling anxious or depressed from their toxicity? Is it really worth having no access to your spiritual guidance?

Junk thoughts come from our programmed, wounded ego mind. These thoughts come from the many false beliefs that we absorbed as we were growing up—such as beliefs about our worth, about what fills us and brings us joy, and about what we can and can't control. Junk thoughts create anxiety, depression, anger, guilt, shame, aloneness, and emptiness, all of which lower your frequency, making it almost impossible to access your Divine guidance.

The Power of Intent Gives Us the Power to Choose

Our intent determines whether we choose junk foods and junk thoughts or healthy foods and thoughts based on truth. Our intent is our highest priority—that is, what is most important to us in any given moment. There are only two intentions available in any given moment:

- the intent to protect against pain with various forms of controlling behavior

- the intent to learn about loving yourself and sharing your love with others

We've all learned many forms of controlling behaviors to avoid feeling our painful feelings. When we were growing up, big pain was too much for our little bodies to manage, so we learned various strategies to avoid feeling our pain. You might have learned any number of these as a child, adolescent, or young adult:

- to dissociate, staying focused in your mind and ignoring your body, where your feelings are

- to judge yourself or to get angry and blame someone else as a way to avoid your painful feelings and to make others responsible for your feelings of worth and safety

- to be compliant by giving yourself up to avoid rejection

- to use substances such as food, alcohol, nicotine, or drugs to numb your pain

- to turn to television, video games, social media, shopping, sex, or porn to distract you from your painful feelings

All these—and many other ways of avoiding responsibility for learning from and taking loving care of your feelings—lower your frequency, making it difficult to connect with your spiritual guidance.

But you now have the choice to open to learning about how to lovingly manage your feelings. You have the choice to learn about what your feelings are telling you and about the beliefs you absorbed that may be limiting you in your work, relationships, and ability to connect with your Divine guidance. All your feelings have vital information for you about whether you are loving yourself and supporting your highest good or whether you are abandoning yourself with your various addictive and controlling behaviors. The more you learn to compassionately open to learning with your feelings and how to heal the false beliefs that are creating much of your pain, the easier it becomes to connect with your spiritual guidance.

Your Intent Determines Your Frequency

Your intent to protect against experiencing and learning from your painful feelings lowers your frequency, while your intent to learn about what your feelings are telling you—and about what is loving to yourself and others—raises your frequency. Learning to lovingly manage your feelings and learn from them, rather than avoid them, is not only vital to attaining at-will Divine connection but is also vital to being able to connect with others and create loving relationships. Abandoning ourselves to our various addictions and controlling behaviors is the major reason for relationship failure.

As you will soon see, becoming aware of your intent and consciously setting the intention to learn, rather than control, is vital for achieving Divine connection. Intent can be a subtle thing, so it's often difficult to be aware of it. Usually the default setting in our brain, which became programmed as we were growing up, is to control in order to try to get love, avoid pain, and feel safe. This is part of our survival mechanism, and it is important to have self-compassion rather than self-judgment for our controlling behavior. We block learning when we judge ourselves. Self-judgment is itself a common form of control and a major way we lower our frequency. We don't learn well when we are anxious as a result of judging ourselves, so practice being accepting and curious about your intent to control as you learn to open to love.

How to Read This Book

I'm excited to share the Inner Bonding process with you. This workbook offers a powerful process for healing the root causes of suffering. It will teach you how to love yourself rather than continue to abandon yourself, how to move beyond emotional dependency and attain emotional freedom, how to heal the underlying control issues—stemming from self-abandonment—that destroy relationships, and how to maintain a strong connection with your personal source of spiritual guidance. It enables you to find and use your inner strength to live life to the fullest, reach your full potential, and become all you are meant to be. The fantastic thing about Inner Bonding is that, because love is the great healer, learning how to love yourself *always works when you do it*.

The six steps of Inner Bonding form a definitive pathway; each step builds up to the next. Therefore, this is not the kind of book in which you can pick a topic you are drawn to. This reading and learning journey unfolds by working through the information and exercises from beginning to end. Once you go through the in-depth version of the method by progressing through this workbook, you will be ready to learn a more consolidated version that you can practice anytime, anywhere. There are also guided meditations and other materials available for download at the website for this book: http://www.newharbinger.com/43188. (See the very back of this book for more details.)

I know that miracles will occur in your life as you learn and practice this profound process, because they happened for me and for thousands of people around the world. So let's embark.

Willing to Feel Pain and Take Responsibility for Your Feelings

In my family, I learned to be a compliant child who took care of everyone else's feelings. I was always vigilantly aware of others' feelings but completely ignored my own, and was therefore unaware of what was going on inside of me. It took me a lot of practice to learn to be present in my body with my feelings. Most of us learned to disconnect from our feelings because we could not manage the pain of abuse, neglect, bullying, rejection, or loss, or of not being seen, valued, and loved in the way we needed. As a result, we also lost access to our gut feelings—our inner knowing, our intuition—as we learned to numb our emotions in order to survive the pain of childhood.

This is why the journey begins by learning to move into the present moment, learning to focus within and tune in to your feelings. It's a choice to be mindful of all your feelings, including your painful ones, rather than protect yourself against them. Honoring yourself in this way helps you want to take responsibility for your feelings, which means that you want to learn about your false beliefs and the self-abandoning behaviors that result. These beliefs and self-rejecting behaviors are the main causes behind anxiety, depression, anger, emptiness, aloneness, guilt, shame, jealousy, and any other wounded feelings. Learning to take responsibility for your feelings allows you to lovingly manage the challenging, painful feelings of life.

Step 1 is about making the decision that you are willing to be present in your body and feel your painful feelings rather than continue to avoid them. My life changed dramatically when I made the decision that *I'm willing to be hurt*. Surprisingly, my willingness to be hurt is one of the major decisions that moved me into a sense of freedom and personal power. As long as I was afraid of getting hurt by people and by life, my intent was to protect against pain. It's when I became willing to be hurt that I became open to learning and to feeling my painful feelings rather than continuing to avoid them. It was this decision that allowed me to get present in my body and reconnect with my feelings.

Step 1 is about practicing moving from mind focus to body focus so that you can be aware of your feelings moment by moment. It offers a mindfulness practice that begins the process of opening you up to receive the positive energy of Spirit that is here to enliven and sustain you. When you reconnect with your feelings, you gain an *inner guidance system* that lets you know about your intent, when you are being loving to yourself, when you are abandoning yourself, what is right for you or wrong for you, and whom you can trust and whom you can't.

Most of us know when we are responsible for a child—our own child or a student or any child temporarily in our care—but many don't believe we are also responsible for caring for our feelings. So it might help you to visualize your feeling self as an inner child who needs your love. But if the term "inner child" doesn't work for you, you can think of your feeling self as your true self, your soul essence, your inner guidance, or whatever else works for you—even just as your feeling self. In the course of this chapter, you will be invited to relate with your inner child through numerous exercises.

First, a word of caution: if you are taking medication for anxiety or depression, and you realize that the meds are numbing your feelings, please don't just stop taking them. As you become able to learn from and lovingly manage your feelings, you need to work with your doctor if you want to gradually get off them.

How We Experience Painful Feelings

Because our feelings are a powerful source of inner guidance, stuffing them away leads to feeling empty and alone and to believing that there is something wrong with us. Here is how Cindy experienced this.

> Cindy is the youngest of three girls. Both her sisters and her father are on the autism spectrum. Her mother is probably not on the spectrum, but she was in her element in a family of people with limited empathy and feelings. By contrast, Cindy is a highly sensitive person and naturally empathic. It was only well into adulthood that she began to understand these differences, but growing up, being so different from the rest of her family, she felt there was something wrong with her. In order to survive, she learned to constantly reject and judge her feelings and then to shut them down completely. By fourteen, she was good at feeling nothing. Being highly sensitive and feeling nothing, Cindy felt she was nothing, and the next twenty years were spent trying to figure out what was wrong.

As children, most people absorbed many fears and beliefs about feelings—beliefs that may have been true as a child but are no longer true now. These beliefs are stored in the lower part of the brain called the amygdala—the part that produces our instinct to fight, flee from, or freeze in the face of danger—and form the basis for your *wounded self*. Your wounded self, or ego, is the part of you that absorbed many fears, false beliefs, and protective behaviors as you were growing up; it can be many different ages, depending on when you experienced painful events or absorbed a false belief.

What fears and beliefs did you absorb as a child about feeling your painful or difficult feelings? What may be blocking you now from feeling? Fears such as *If I open up to my pain, it will never end*, or *If I feel that much pain, people will notice it and judge me, and I will end up alone*, or *If I don't block my pain, I won't be able to function*, or *I will go crazy or die if I feel my painful feelings*.

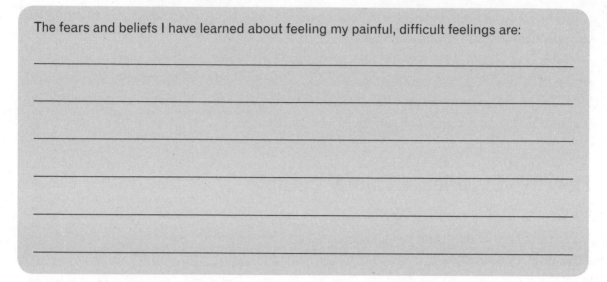

The fears and beliefs I have learned about feeling my painful, difficult feelings are:

_____

_____

_____

_____

_____

_____

Look at each of the fears and beliefs you wrote down. Are they still true today as an adult? If you think they are, put an X beside them. If you can see that they are not still true and that they are allowing your wounded self to scare you and block your feelings, put a check mark beside them. You can revisit this list as you journey through this workbook to check in with yourself about how these fears and beliefs might be evolving.

Distinguishing Wounded Feelings from the Pain of Life

We all have two different kinds of painful feelings. When our intent is to control, and we are avoiding responsibility for our feelings, painful *wounded feelings* result, such as anxiety, depression, guilt, shame, anger, aloneness, emptiness, and jealousy. These are created by us when we abandon ourselves.

The *pain of life* is core pain or existential pain, such as grief, loneliness, heartbreak, sorrow, fear of real and present danger, outrage over injustice, helplessness over others' unloving behavior, and other emotional responses to major losses and traumatic life events. As children, we could not manage the existential pain of life, so we learned to stuff away our feelings, which we did by developing controlling and avoidant survival strategies. Now, as adults, learning to lovingly manage the deeper pain of life is vital, because avoiding this pain leads to protective, controlling, avoidant behavior and to various forms of self-abandonment, such as

- staying focused in your head, ignoring your feelings

- judging yourself

- turning to substance and process addictions—such as addictions to work, television, shopping, sex—to numb and avoid your feelings, and

- making others responsible for your feelings.

Distinguishing painful wounded feelings from existential pain is about understanding which are painful feelings you create with your self-abandonment and which are the result of life situations and experiences outside of your control.

Let's say someone you are close with yells at you or judges you. It generally feels hurtful when people are unloving to us, so you might feel the loneliness and heartache of being treated poorly. And because you have no control over others' feelings and behavior, you might feel the difficult feeling of being helpless in the face of their abusive behavior. This is *existential pain*—pain that is being caused by something external to you. But if you then blame yourself for their unloving behavior (if you think to yourself something like, *They wouldn't say these things if I didn't deserve it*), you might feel anger, guilt, or shame. This is *wounded pain*—pain that is caused internally by your self-abandonment.

Here's another example: say some friends you love die in a car accident. You feel grief, loneliness, heartbreak, and helplessness over their deaths. This is existential pain—the pain of loss. But if you then ruminate about how you shouldn't have let them drive at that time, or that you should have known ahead of time that something bad was going to happen, you might feel depressed, angry, or guilty. This is wounded pain—pain that results from the false beliefs of the wounded self.

Let's explore more about the challenging and painful existential feelings of life. Here are ways you might experience them.

Loneliness: You might feel lonely when you want to share love with someone, and there is no one there to share it with, or the people who are there are not open to sharing love or connection. Loneliness is different than *aloneness*, which you will feel when you are abandoning yourself. Rejecting and abandoning ourselves results in feeling alone and empty inside. If you are abandoning yourself, you might feel both alone and lonely, because you can't connect with others and share love when you are disconnected from yourself due to self-rejection and self-abandonment.

Heartache, sorrow, and *heartbreak*: You might feel heartbroken over any number of experiences—losing a loved one, losing a job you loved, being treated badly, seeing people or animals being abused, seeing friends you care about treating themselves badly, or seeing the damaged state of our planet. We may feel sorrow when we see people hurting each other or hurting the planet.

Grief: You feel grief when you lose someone or something you love—a parent, a partner, a child, an animal, a home, and so on.

Helpless over others: You feel helpless when others are behaving in ways that hurt you, hurt themselves, or hurt others.

Outrage: Anger over injustice moves you to take loving action for yourself or others. Anger can also blame others when you are actually rejecting or abandoning yourself and *projecting* it onto others. We will explore the issue of projecting in depth during step 3.

Fear of real and present danger: This is the fight-or-flight urge we feel when we are in immediate danger—like if we are attacked by a mugger. Sometimes we can sense this danger a little ahead of time, and it's important to heed this instinct. This fear is different than our wounded self projecting bad things—things that can or might happen—into the future. Eliza's story illustrates this difference.

> *Eliza had dropped her fourteen-year-old daughter off at a friend's house and was spending some much-needed time alone in her house. But after about an hour, she suddenly had a feeling of dread. Fortunately, she listened to her feeling and quickly drove back to the friend's house. When she didn't find her daughter there, she went next door, knowing that the boy next door was a friend of her daughter's friend. She discovered that there was a group of boys there who were attempting to rape her daughter and her friend. She was able to stop them and called the police. As she told me this, tears of gratitude were rolling down her cheeks that she had listened to her inner guidance.*

We can feel more than one of these existential pains at a time—we can feel lonely, heartbroken, helpless over others and events, and grief all at once. These feelings are hard to experience, which is why we learned to avoid them as we were growing up. You might find that you judge yourself or ruminate to avoid the existential pain of life—adding wounded pain to the existential pain—or that you turn to various substances or activities to avoid the pain, rather than compassionately feeling it and allowing it to move through you each time it comes up. *Addictions are a way to avoid these painful feelings.* This keeps you stuck in both existential pain and wounded pain.

Your feelings always have profound and unerring information for you. For example, when you feel anxious, this might be telling you that you are judging yourself or that an old, unhealed trauma is being triggered. Or it might be telling you that your gut flora is out of balance, creating a toxicity that then goes into your brain. In all of these cases, the anxiety is likely telling you that you are abandoning yourself in some way—emotionally, physically, or by not doing the healing work of the past you need to do.

Burying your feelings in any way can be harmful to your health, which is what happened to Rosanna.

"You've got cancer, but don't worry too much about it. We can operate to remove the tumor from your throat. Perhaps chemotherapy afterward. I hope I won't damage your vocal chords during the operation. I see in my file that you're a teacher. Hmm, so you will need your voice. Still, your vocal chords might get damaged. Well, we need to operate quickly."

This is what the surgeon told Rosanna more than twenty years ago. It wasn't the surgeon's lack of sensitivity that she found most disturbing—it was her passivity, her smiling in silence, swallowing her pain and fear, and hiding her desperation. At that time no one—not the surgeon, not her general practitioner or the nurses in the hospital, not her colleagues or her family or her friends—was ever to know how she felt.

"This is how I was treating myself at the time: total non-validation of my feelings. This is what I had learned growing up: an unwritten rule that 'feeling' was a taboo subject. You never voiced your feelings, and if you did, it resulted in ridicule, shaming, blaming, and ignoring. No wonder I had become an expert at it."

The journey of her recovery was twofold: her physical body healed, but that wasn't enough. She also needed to heal her inner child, her feeling self. She started reading up on cancer and learned that negative feelings, if pushed away and buried long enough, can manifest as malignant tumors. This is when she learned to speak up for herself.

When your inner child feels abandoned by you, he or she might not cause actual illness but might cause physical pain as a way to get your attention. Such was the case with David.

Since David was a teenager, he suffered from serious migraine headaches and regularly took strong medication for relief. As he began to develop a relationship with his inner child, he noticed a lessening of inner tension, and the frequency and intensity of the headaches diminished. For the last twelve years, he has seldom had a headache.

Becoming aware of your feelings is an essential first step for Divine connection. Painful, wounded feelings—or any lack of inner peace—let you know that you are abandoning yourself, while peaceful feelings let you know that you are loving yourself. When you learn to lovingly manage the existential pains of life, you can even learn to stay inwardly peaceful in the face of losses and others' unloving behavior.

Is there current or past pain from your life experiences that you are trying to avoid by covering them over with self-judgments, substance addictions, or addictions to activities? Write a list of any painful feelings you are aware of. Then, see if you can distinguish between the wounded pain and the pain of life that you might be avoiding.

_____

_____

_____

_____

Learning to Lovingly Manage Existential Pain

There are five major reasons why it is vitally important to learn to lovingly manage your existential pain:

- Releasing the feelings rather than keeping them stuck in your body promotes good health. As we've seen, stuck feelings cause stress, which often leads to illness.

- Addictions are a way of avoiding these feelings, so the more you learn to lovingly release them, the more your addiction to substances, activities, and processes will heal.

- You won't get stuck with the wounded feelings of anxiety, depression, anger, guilt, and shame that may be covering up the deeper, painful feelings of life.

- Both pain and joy exist in the same place in the heart. You can't numb out to the painful feelings of life without also limiting the wonderful feelings of life—love, compassion, peace, and joy. If you want to experience the joy of life, you need to learn to lovingly manage the pain of life.

• Knowledge of your passion and purpose is within your soul self. When you avoid existential pain with self-abandoning behavior, you block access to your deeper sense of purpose, which can lead you to wondering why you are on the planet.

Many of the people I work with discover their passionate purpose as they learn to lovingly manage their existential pain, which creates the sense of safety your inner child needs to let you in on why you are on the planet. This is exactly what occurred with Rachel.

One of Rachel's dreams as a girl had been to study psychology, but she was told to "learn something sensible" instead. She obliged and became a secondary school teacher. As a young adult, it never occurred to her to ask her inner child what her dream or passion was. Years later, as a woman in her late forties, she learned to listen to her inner guidance and took loving action by enrolling in school to study psychology. Once she had uncovered the lies her wounded self had been telling her, and once she stopped numbing her uncomfortable feelings, she was able to fulfill her dreams and passion.

Here is a meditation you can do to practice offering your hurting inner child more love and compassion.

Take some deep, mindful breaths and tune in to any current or past loneliness, grief, heartbreak, or feelings of helplessness over others.

Put your hands on your heart to help you keep your focus in your heart and to stimulate oxytocin, often called the "love hormone."

Visualize bringing love and compassion inside to where you feel the existential pain. Gently and tenderly say out loud to your inner child, "I'm here with you. You are not alone. Spirit is here—we are not alone. I will stay with you for as long as you need me."

Let yourself cry if tears come up. Stay with the feelings until you feel a release inside, and then visualize the feelings being released from your body. Say, "I release these feelings, and open to peace and acceptance."

The pain may come up over and over. Do this each time it comes up.

Accessing Your Feelings

While we are often taught how to not feel things by staying in our head, we are rarely taught how to engage our body so that feelings can safely surface. Here is a process you can do anytime—now and throughout your life—to access your feelings.

If you have suffered severe physical, sexual, or emotional abuse, you need support when opening to your feelings. You were alone the first time you were so deeply hurt, and being alone now isn't loving to yourself. You need a compassionate therapist, facilitator, coach, or loving friend to be with you as you open to your old pain. You need to go slowly, dipping in just a little at a time. Plunging into your feelings can leave you flooded and overwhelmed by the pain. There is no rush.

Use your breath to get present in your body, taking some deep, mindful breaths, paying attention to the sensations of your breath as it moves in and out of your body.

Emotions are often linked with physical sensations, so scan your body downward from head to toes and notice any tension, tightness, unease, emptiness, numbness, fluttering, or pain. If your inner feeling self—your inner child—hasn't been able to get your attention, he or she may be using physical pain to send you a message. Breathe into these sensations, getting fully present with them. Don't worry if you don't feel anything or if you can't identify your feelings. Sometimes it takes time for your inner child to feel safe enough to let you in. Perhaps right now all you can tune in to is whether you feel good or bad.

If you can access your feelings, see if you can name an emotion, such as anxiety, anger, depression, emptiness, aloneness, or loneliness. If you can't name the emotion, don't worry about it. It's often enough just to know when you are feeling anything less than peaceful within. Be aware that numbness isn't the same as peace. Peace is a calm feeling of fullness within, while numbness is often an empty feeling—feeling nothing.

What are you feeling inside right now?

_____

_____

_____

Become fully present with your feelings, moving toward them rather than away from them, and embrace them with kindness and openness rather than judging them or doing any other forms of self-abandonment to avoid them.

What else do you feel when you kindly and gently get present in your body with your feelings?

_____

_____

_____

_____

Learning to stay present in your body and wanting to take responsibility for your feelings takes much practice. Since most of us learned to stay in our head as a way of avoiding our pain, remembering to stay present in your body can be a challenge.

When I started to engage this process thirty-four years ago, I was totally in my head. I found it hard to even remember to notice my own feelings, so I needed a reminder. I used a little gadget (a MotivAider) that would silently buzz against my body. I started out setting it to buzz every five minutes to remind me to check inside by body. Then I went to every ten minutes, then every thirty minutes. I wore it until I had trained myself to stay present in my body.

You can set an alert on your cell phone, put sticky notes in places where you will see them regularly, wear a rubber band that you can snap to remind yourself, or use something like a MotivAider. The main challenge in getting present in your body is remembering to do so. Most of us are deeply programmed to immediately avoid our feelings by using an addictive, controlling behavior, such as grazing from the refrigerator, judging ourselves or someone else, or yelling at the dog. It takes time and practice to remember to get present in your body rather than trying to avoid experiencing and taking responsibility for your feelings.

Awareness of How You Avoid Your Feelings

We've all learned many addictive and other self-abandoning ways of avoiding our feelings. So please try to be both kind and honest with yourself as you go through this exercise. No self-judgment! Remember, most of us never learned how to learn from our pain and lovingly take responsibility for our feelings, so avoiding your feelings has been the best you could do. However, everything you do to avoid your pain lowers your frequency and makes it hard to access your Divine guidance.

Breathe in and take a few minutes to start to tune in to the various ways you try to avoid your painful feelings.

What substances—such as junk food, sugar, alcohol, drugs, or nicotine—do you use to avoid your painful feelings and taking responsibility for them?

_____

_____

_____

_____

What activities—such as spending, shopping, cleaning, cluttering, work, television, porn, sex, video games, gambling, using social media or the Internet, busyness, or over-exercising—do you use to avoid your feelings and taking responsibility for them? Using activities to avoid your feelings can be addictive. For example, you can use meditation to get centered and connect, or you can use it to bliss out and avoid responsibility for your feelings. You can watch television to relax and enjoy your favorite program or just to numb yourself. It depends on your intent. What activities to you generally use to avoid your feelings?

_____

_____

_____

_____

What controlling behaviors do you turn to—such as blaming, anger, rage, threats, withdrawal, resistance, or compliance (giving yourself up)—to avoid feeling and taking responsibility for your feelings?

_____

_____

_____

_____

What other forms of self-rejection and self-abandonment do you turn to, to avoid your existential pain, such as self-judgment, self-criticism, worrying, obsessive thinking, complaining, or staying focused in your mind rather than in your body with your feelings?

_____

_____

_____

_____

Do you act out painful feelings rather than expressing them directly? Acting out would include expressing anger and rage, throwing tantrums, threatening, behaving in a passive-aggressive manner, engaging in risky activities or self-destructive behavior like cutting, and trolling on social media.

_____

_____

_____

_____

Right now, just for this moment, practice accepting responsibility for your feelings. Move toward them with kindness and gentleness. Imagine sitting with your inner child in your lap, cuddled in your arms, and say, "Right now, in this moment, I'm here with you. You are not alone and I'm not going to leave you." Imagine there is a loving presence holding you as you hold your inner child. Breathe, and be with that for a few minutes.

Being willing to become aware of your feelings, face them, and accept them can open up new possibilities in life. Because we are no longer driven by avoidance, which leads to painful situations in addition to painful feelings, we can truly be with ourselves and with others. Carolynn learned this when she looked deeper into her feelings about her boss.

Periodically in her life, Carolynn has found herself strongly drawn to people who have some element in common with her dysfunctional family, and who tend to bring out both her best and worst. This was the case with her boss. As much as she wanted to work with this man, at first she was triggered and swept up in overwhelming feelings resulting from seemingly simple interactions. Carolynn also felt a powerful physical attraction to him, which was a dangerous situation in a job she loved. As she worked through a lot of primal and visceral painful feelings from her childhood, Carolynn was stunned to see that she sometimes thought of her boss as responsible for these feelings. The existential pains she felt were hard for her to acknowledge, let alone accept, but she was eventually able to honor them and learn what they were telling her about the false beliefs she acquired as she was growing up. Her process led to the discovery that the deeper painful feelings could be resolved, including a natural resolution of the physical attraction, without anything happening between them. The result: Carolynn and her boss have enjoyed working closely for many years now and have a healthy and professional working relationship. Together, they lead a great team.

Carolynn turned what could have been a disastrous situation—if she had reacted in a way that cost her a job—into something positive. She did this by taking responsibility for her feelings.

Deepening Responsibility for Your Feelings

Most parents are role models for how to avoid your feelings—blaming someone or something for them, turning to addictions to avoid them, or dissociating to numb themselves. Our culture fosters the belief that we are the victims of our feelings and should expect others to fix them. Can you think of anyone, other than the Dalai Lama, who takes 100 percent responsibility for his or her feelings, never blaming others? The Dalai Lama is a wonderful role model for this practice. By taking responsibility for his feelings, he is a joyous man, despite the many painful challenges he has had in his life.

Did your parents or other caregivers model taking responsibility for their feelings? Did you ever hear them say, in response to their wounded feelings, "I wonder what I'm thinking and how I'm treating myself that is causing me to feel badly right now?" Did you ever see them nurturing themselves in response to their existential pain? Probably not.

> What did your parents model for you as you were growing up?
>
> _____
>
> _____
>
> _____

Most of us grew up with many false beliefs that today prevent us from taking responsibility for our own feelings. Perhaps you believe that if no one loved you as you were growing up, it's up to someone else to do it now. Or perhaps, because your parents were overprotective and did everything for you, you think that it's someone else's job to give you happiness and a sense of worth. Maybe you believe that you must be needy in order to attract a partner or that if you learn to take loving care of your feelings, you won't want a partner. Your wounded self may have many false beliefs that are blocking you from taking responsibility for your feelings, but it is accepting that responsibility that allows you to learn what you are doing to cause the wounded feelings and helps you lovingly manage the existential pains of life.

> If you feel resistance to taking responsibility for your feelings, identify the fears and beliefs causing the resistance. Take some time to honestly go within. Why don't you want to take this responsibility?
>
> _____
>
> _____
>
> _____
>
> _____
>
> _____
>
> _____

Sometimes people do want to heal, but because they have no idea how to take responsibility for their feelings, they do what they've learned to do, which is to keep avoiding them with their addictions. Even if they reach out for help, they often don't get what they need, which was my experience with the many therapists I saw—and which was the case for Henry.

Henry started using alcohol and drugs when he was twelve, and by the time he was fourteen, he was shooting heroin. As a teen, he dropped out of school, thinking he was stupid. He had no close relationships and couldn't hold down a job. He suffered from severe depression and finally, after twenty years of drug and alcohol abuse, decided to get treatment.

He went to outpatient and inpatient detox programs numerous times and had various forms of therapy, but because no one ever helped him address the painful childhood issues that led to his substance abuse, or taught him how to take responsibility for his feelings, he always went back to getting high. After being diagnosed with hepatitis C and starting to have suicidal thoughts, he ended up in the psychiatric unit of his local hospital. He worked with a psychiatrist but, again, didn't receive the help he needed.

Still suffering from depression, he was in and out of mental health centers. He sought relief by going to church and tried Hinduism, Buddhism, Scientology, and meditation. All of this offered some relief, but nothing substantial.

After being accepted by a new state health care plan for the poor and chronically ill, he was told that he had end-stage cirrhosis of the liver and that if he didn't get a transplant, he would be dead within a year. He got on the organ-donor waiting list for a liver, and nine months later, when he was in the emergency room suffering from liver failure, he got the call that a donor had been found.

After surgery, the side effects of the antirejection injections he needed caused suicidal and homicidal thoughts. This led him back to the mental health center, where he was treated by another therapist who, fortunately, had been trained in Inner Bonding and who, at last, helped Henry discover that he was treating himself the way his profoundly neglectful mother and his severely emotionally abusive father and older brother had treated him. Gradually, Henry learned to see himself for the smart, creative, and sensitive person he is and began to take loving care of himself.

Currently, Henry no longer suffers from depression and is now able to truly share love with others. He went back to school, did well, and is now self-supporting. His physical condition has been stable for ten years since his transplant.

Like so many of the people I work with, Henry was a sensitive child, and the only way he knew to manage the intense pain of his childhood was to numb himself with substances. It's not that he didn't want responsibility—it's that he had no idea that he was responsible for his feelings and no idea how to take this responsibility. One of the major reasons we need at-will access to our Divine guidance is because it models for us how to take loving responsibility for our feelings—and for our lives.

Using Spirituality to Avoid Feelings

We can even use our spirituality to avoid responsibility for embracing and learning from our feelings. This has been called "spiritual bypassing," and it can be a source of many personal and relationship problems within spiritual communities. Larissa's story is an illustration of how even a person who grew up with loving parents and a spiritual connection can do a spiritual bypass rather than take responsibility for her feelings.

Larissa grew up in a loving home with parents who were spiritual seekers, so when she was twelve years old, she learned to meditate. Since then, she always felt that her inner connection with Spirit was her source of meaning and strength. Unfortunately, somewhere along the way, she learned to devalue her feelings. She would judge what she called her "weaknesses and foibles"—which often were her feelings of depression, aloneness, and loneliness—against an idealized version of what it meant to be spiritual. Larissa berated herself for her coffee habit, told herself she was a terrible practitioner whenever she felt angry, and was upset that her body never looked as good as others' in her yoga classes. In the midst of striving for her version of an ideal spiritual state, she had left her inner child far behind.

When at last she opened to her feelings, she cried and felt more loneliness than she could remember in her previous forty-six years. At the same time, she said, "It is a strange paradox that I have never felt better. It seems true that by pushing down the difficult painful feelings, I diminished my ability to experience the wonderful feelings too."

I once received an email from a man who had been studying spirituality and meditating for over twenty years. He was high-ranking member of a well-known spiritual center and was also a teacher at that center. But he had begun to feel suicidal, and he realized that while meditating, he had been explaining away his feelings, trying to rise above them, and hoping that they would eventually just go away as he reached higher transcendent states. His inner child was so miserable at having his feelings ignored for so long that he wanted off the planet. He shared with me that as soon as he started to compassionately attend to his feelings and learn from them, as you will learn to do in this workbook, his suicidal feelings disappeared.

When You Need to Reach Out for Help

Sometimes painful feelings can overwhelm our capacity to be present for ourselves, and if that happens, we need to reach out for help. Being lovingly held by a nurturing person, someone who has no agenda other than to be a channel of Divine Love for you, is extremely healing. Growing up, many of us didn't receive the nurturing we needed when we were in pain. So receiving this nurturing now heals on a deep, core level. The person holding you and nurturing you can be a man or a woman, but not someone you are in a romantic or sexual relationship with. Just as a child needs loving attention and is traumatized by sexual abuse, your inner child needs the pure energy of nurturing without any other agenda attached to it.

Old pain is healed as you learn to show up for your current and past feelings with compassion and kindness. But you can't always do it by yourself. We all need help with deep pain. Asking for help isn't the same as abandoning yourself. If you want to be loving to your inner child, but the feelings are too big and overwhelming, asking for help from a loving adult is part of being a loving adult for yourself. Just make sure that you are not asking this person to take responsibility for your feelings—that you are asking them to do it *with* you, not *for* you.

Becoming aware of feelings and taking responsibility for them is a surefire way of becoming aware of your intent, which is essential for Divine connection.

Step 2

Move into the Intent to Learn

You have learned that you need to practice becoming present with your feelings, and hopefully, you have decided that you want responsibility for them. Now it is time to consciously choose the intent to learn about loving yourself and inviting the compassionate presence of Spirit into your heart. Your intent is your deepest desire, your primary motivation. As I stated in the introduction, there are only two possible intentions you can have in any given moment: the intent to protect yourself from pain and the intent to learn about loving yourself. In this step, you will explore becoming your loving adult self.

When you have the intent to learn about loving yourself and you are connected with the love and wisdom of your Divine guidance, you are operating as a loving adult. When you are in the intent to protect, control, and avoid, you are operating from your wounded self. The loving adult is the emissary of Spirit, taking loving actions that are guided by Spirit—actions on your behalf and on behalf of others.

We all grow up to be adults, but unfortunately, many of us don't grow up to be loving adults. Since most of our parents were operating from their wounded selves, few of us had good role models. And since there are not many role models in our society either, we need to be able to turn to our Divine guidance to learn how to love ourselves.

Since the vast majority of us automatically and unconsciously choose the intent to control when feeling fearful or stressed, becoming aware of our intent and our ability to choose it can be a major challenge. It takes practice, especially when we are triggered into fear or stress. So we begin by becoming aware that we are actually *choosing* our intention.

Take a few deep breaths, breathing deeply inside. Mindfully follow your breath as it goes in and out of your body. Move out of mind focus, and bring your focus inside your body, becoming fully present in your body.

As you tune in to your body, notice whether you feel like a happy puppy or a grumpy cat. (My wonderful cat is never grumpy, but when I think of a grumpy cat, I think of a scared stray cat.) A happy puppy is open, friendly, expansive, and spontaneous, while a grumpy cat is inward, sullen, threatening, angry, and shut down, and might hiss or scratch someone.

The challenge is in recognizing that you are *choosing* to be a happy puppy or a grumpy cat. Without any judgment, write down whether you are currently, in this moment, closed, controlling, and avoiding—or open to learning about loving yourself and others.

_____

_____

Changing Your Intent from Controlling to Loving

If your current intent is to control and avoid, don't worry. With practice, it's possible to make a conscious decision regarding whether you want to continue to attempt to control a person or situation and to avoid your feelings, or whether you want to open to learning about loving yourself and others. Since we have free will, we can learn to choose our intention *moment by moment*.

To get the most out of using this workbook, you might want to consciously choose the intent to learn when you are doing this inner work. Since it takes much practice to *stay* in the intent to learn, especially around challenging people and situations, your choice is always for right now, in this moment.

Right now, I am choosing my intent. It is to:

_____

_____

Becoming Aware of Your Intent with Others

When your intent is to control, which is what activates your wounded self with all its fears and false beliefs, other people might feel threatening to you, even when they are happy puppies. When your intent is to love, even if the other people are grumpy cats, you can learn—with practice—to keep your heart open to loving yourself and them. While it might seem that your only choice is to be reactive when others are being unloving to you, others don't determine your intent. You are the only one in charge of your intent.

Think about the important people in your life and what your intent generally is with each of them. If your intent is generally to control, write what fears might be in the way of being open to learning.

When I'm with _____, generally my intent is

_____

If my intent is generally to control, what are the fears of being open to learning?

_____

When I'm with _____, generally my intent is

_____

If my intent is generally to control, what are the fears of being open to learning?

_____

When I'm with _____, generally my intent is

_____

If my intent is generally to control, what are the fears of being open to learning?

_____

When I'm with _____, generally my intent is

_____

If my intent is generally to control, what are the fears of being open to learning?

_____

Consciously Choosing the Intent to Learn

When we choose the intent to learn, we become open to learning about our various forms of self-abandonment, our false and limiting beliefs, where we got these beliefs, what is true regarding our false beliefs, responses that are loving to ourselves, and skills that act in our highest good. We feel kind and compassionate toward our feelings, rather than judgmental. We know that we have good reasons for our feelings and behavior—which are our programmed fears and false beliefs—and we want to learn about them to heal them.

This starts with learning to love yourself and fill yourself with love. You can't share your love with others unless you have love to share. Choosing the intent to learn is choosing to learn to love yourself. Take a moment to make this choice.

Become present in your body with your feelings, and decide that you want responsibility for your feelings. Then put your hands on your heart, focusing your attention in your heart, and taking some deep, mindful breaths while visualizing space opening up in your heart.

Once you feel centered, say out loud, "I consciously choose the intent to learn about loving myself."

Once you feel this choice in your heart, invite the presence of love and compassion to arise within your heart by simply saying, "I invite you into my heart." This is the loving presence of your higher self.

Feelings of love and compassion aren't generated just from within ourselves; we open to them and invite them in. Love and compassion, as well as peace and joy, are gifts of Spirit. They *are* Spirit, and, because we have free will, they enter our beings only by invitation. Choosing the intent to learn about loving yourself is the invitation Spirit needs to fill you. When you become open to learning about love and feel connected with your higher source of love, you will operate as a loving adult.

For a moment, imagine being a loving adult to an actual child. Think about the safety you need to create for a child to feel comfortable enough to let you close. If you were to approach an anxious child from your wounded self with a harsh voice—saying something like, "What's the matter with you now?"—the child would not feel safe enough to let you in. But if you approached the child as a loving adult, compassionately saying, "Sweetie, you seem upset. Do you want to tell me all about it?" the child would likely be able to open up to you, even if he or she was upset with you.

It's the same with your inner child. You need to be a loving adult for your inner child to feel safe enough to let you in. So let's deepen the process of becoming this source of safety and compassion.

It may not be easy to be honest with yourself regarding your current intent. The wounded self wants you to think you are open when you are actually closed. Do the best you can to be honest with yourself as you answer the following questions to help you discern your intent.

Ask yourself these questions and check off what is true for you:

_____   Do I currently believe others are causing my feelings and behavior—that I'm a victim of others' choices?

_____ Do I currently believe that I can control others' feelings or behavior?

_____ Am I judging myself or others as right or wrong, good or bad?

_____ Am I currently closed to my Divine guidance?

_____ Am I willing to give myself up by sacrificing my true self, rather than speak my truth and risk losing another?

_____ Am I attaching my worth and happiness to the outcome?

_____ Do I believe I can control the outcome?

_____ Am I avoiding responsibility for my feelings with addictive, controlling behaviors?

_____ Am I primarily trying to get love and avoid pain? Am I mainly interested in getting rid of pain?

Answering yes to any of these questions likely indicates that your intent is to protect, avoid, and control. If this is the case, please don't judge yourself. Remember, we are all deeply programmed to operate from our wounded ego with the intent to control. And remember that there are always good reasons for wanting to control rather than learn. Being aware of your intent to control is important in terms of being able to choose the intent to learn. You can't open to learning if you believe you are open when you are actually closed and protecting yourself against pain.

Ask yourself these questions and check off what is true for you:

_____ Am I feeling kindly and compassionate toward my feelings?

_____ Do I have a deep desire to take responsibility for my own feelings and behavior?

_____ Do I accept that I and others have good reasons—our programmed fears and false beliefs—for our feelings and behavior?

_____ Am I genuinely curious about discovering my fears and false beliefs that are limiting me and causing my wounded pain?

_____ Am I connected with the love and wisdom of my higher self?

_____ Am I willing to be honest with myself without self-judgment, and am I willing to tell my total truth with others without blame or judgment?

_____ Am I willing to risk losing others by speaking and acting from my truth, rather than lose myself by giving myself up and complying with what another wants?

_____ Is it more important to me to be loving than to protect against my fears of anger, judgment, rejection, failure, hurt, being controlled, and so on?

_____ Is it more important to me to be loving than to attempt to control others into making me feel temporarily safe, loved, happy, understood, adequate, or worthy?

_____ Am I willing to learn about loving myself, even in the face of fear?

Answering yes to these indicates that your intent is to learn about loving yourself and others. I know this is a lot, so again, be sure not to judge yourself if you can't answer yes to these questions in this moment. And remember, this is a moment-by-moment choice, so if it feels too challenging to be open to learning right now, that could change later today or tomorrow or the next day. This is a learning process, and it takes much practice to be open to learning about loving yourself most of the time. If you could stay open all the time, you would be an enlightened being!

Since most if not all of us have been practicing being in the intent to protect, avoid, and control for most of our lives, even remembering to choose the intent to learn is a big challenge. We don't choose this once, and that's it. Given that we have free will, we get to choose our intent each moment, and everything else follows from our intent. As I've previously stated, choosing our intent is the essence of free will.

Being open to learning isn't about waiting until you heal your fears. It's about choosing to learn what you are doing to cause your pain, what your false beliefs are, and what is loving to you, *even in the face of fear.*

This is what courage is all about. The loving adult is about choosing the spiritual path of love and courage, rather than the earthly path of fear, which is the path of the wounded self. The LifePaths Chart shows you the choices and consequences of each path. You can find it on New Harbinger's website, at **http://www.newharbinger.com/43188.**

Discerning Between Being Open and Acting Open

The wounded self can be tricky; it often acts like it knows what it's talking about, when it's actually making up lies and saying them with a voice of authority. It wants you to think it's powerful, so it talks in a loud voice. It might help you to think of the wounded self as a child or adolescent with a megaphone. The voice of Spirit, on the other hand, is generally quiet, so it might seem easier to listen to the loud, authoritative, and controlling voice of the wounded self. But do you want a child or adolescent in charge of your life?

Tune in to your heart. Does your heart *feel* open and expansive, or is it constricted? Your body might be tense, because there may be feelings you need to deal with, but if you are open to learning, your heart will feel open.

_____

_____

You might find it fairly easy to be open to learning with yourself, but what about being open to learning with another person, especially in conflict? We will be exploring loving actions in relationship conflict in step 5, but for now, it's important for you to be able to discern only whether you are truly open with another person or simply acting open.

Bring to mind a situation in which you are in conflict with another person. Whether the conflict is big or small, choose a situation in which the issue or the person is challenging you.

Mark the following questions yes or no.

_____ Are you hoping that by discussing a current conflict, the other person will hear you and change?

_____ Are you obsessing about what you want to say to them to get them to see things your way?

_____ Are you hoping that if they see things your way they will apologize to you?

_____ Do you believe that one of you is right and one of you is wrong, and that the other person is wrong?

_____ Is it more important to you to be right and win than it is to learn?

_____ Are you trying to "make nice" so that the other person won't be mad at you?

If you answered yes to any of the above, it's likely that your wounded self is merely acting open, and that you are not truly open to learning about yourself and about the other person.

Being honest with yourself, answer the following questions: Why do you want to talk about the conflict? What is your hope in talking about it?

_____

_____

_____

_____

Again, mark the following questions yes or no.

_____ If you are considering exploring a conflict with another person, do you feel curious about your part of the conflict and about the good reasons they have for feeling and behaving as they are?

_____ Do you feel that you can support your own highest good as well as the other person's highest good?

_____ Is it important to you to reach an understanding of yourself and the other person?

_____ Are you aiming for a win-win conflict resolution, in which you both feel heard and understood, and you come up with a resolution that you are both happy with?

_____ Are you prepared to take loving care of yourself if the other person isn't open to learning with you?

If you answered yes to these questions, then you are likely open to learning with the other person.

Ultimately, your feelings will tell you about your intent. When you are a loving adult open to learning, you will feel a peacefulness and sense of safety inside. When your wounded self is in charge, regardless of how adept your wounded self is at acting open, you will feel some stress and a lack of inner safety.

Working with Anger

Most people never learned healthy ways of learning from and managing anger.

> What do you generally do when you are angry? How do you express anger? Do you dump it on someone else or shove it inside?
>
> _____
>
> _____
>
> _____

Like all our wounded feelings, anger has important information for us regarding how we are abandoning ourselves. Anger at another person is generally your inner child's anger at you for not taking loving care of yourself—anger that is projected onto someone else. Recognizing your anger at others as a projection is how you can take responsibility for it, and this moves you into an intent to learn.

As I stated earlier, there are two kinds of anger: outrage and blaming anger. Since this is an important concept, I will repeat the definitions to show the difference between adult outrage and anger coming from the wounded self.

Outrage is the anger that comes from a loving adult in response to injustice, such as seeing someone hurting a child, an animal, the environment, and so on. It is the kind of anger that moves us to take loving action for ourselves and for others.

This kind of anger is important. It focuses us and mobilizes us into taking necessary action. This is not the anger of a victim. Rather, it is the anger that comes from a place of personal power.

Blaming anger comes from the wounded self and is a form of control and avoidance. You might hope to intimidate others into doing what you want or into believing what you want them to believe. It's also a way to avoid the painful feeling of helplessness over others.

Blaming anger is often our reaction to fear and comes from feeling like a victim. When our fears of being hurt, rejected, alone, abandoned, smothered, or controlled are triggered, we may protect against these fears by getting angry at whoever is activating them. Our hope is that the other person will stop the threatening behavior.

Since helplessness is such a difficult feeling, being helpless over another's behavior often activates our desire to be in control. Yet the reality is that we are helpless over what others choose to do and how they feel about us. When we don't accept the truth of our helplessness over others, we may continue to attempt to control them with anger.

Sometimes we get angry in the hopes that others will change if they see how hurt we are by their behavior or that they will at least apologize and feel compassion for us. The problem is that often the other person feels hurt or threatened by our anger and, instead of caring about us, goes into his or her own reactive behavior—anger, withdrawal, or resistance. Our blaming anger can set into motion a negative cycle of behavior that ends with both people feeling awful.

People who use blaming anger as a form of control often feel justified in getting angry: "Don't I have a right to get angry if someone hurts me or disrespects me?" The problem is that the anger itself is hurtful and disrespectful; it is fighting fire with fire, which may backfire!

The question is not whether or not you have a right to be angry. The questions to ask are: Is getting angry at someone serving you well? Is it really getting you what you want? Is anger at someone else really the best way of taking care of yourself? Your wounded self may say, "Yes! I feel much better when I get my anger out." That may be true for the moment—addictions always feel good in the moment, which is why they become addictions. But does your angry behavior enhance your self-esteem, your feelings of self-worth, your inner sense of safety and security? Often the opposite is true: angry behavior may increase feelings of shame and insecurity. When we behave in unloving ways toward others, we cannot help but end up feeling unlovable.

My angry behavior makes me feel:

_____

_____

_____

Since not everyone uses anger as a protection against their deeper pain, anger work isn't for everyone. But if you find your openness blocked by anger, you need a powerful way to unblock it. Whenever we get angry at others because they hurt us, we are making them responsible for our feelings. We are being a victim, blaming others for our hurt and anger. There is no loving adult taking responsibility for our own feelings and behavior—there is just a wounded child acting out.

Releasing your anger will work only when your intent in releasing it is to learn about what you are doing that is causing your angry feelings. If you just want to use your anger to blame, control, and justify your position, you will stay stuck in your anger, stuck with a closed heart. In fact, dumping out your anger often generates even more anger. When people dump their anger on others or vent their anger by pounding pillows with their fists or with a bat—with no learning or personal responsibility for their feelings—no healing occurs. This dumping or venting keeps you stuck as a victim.

The Anger Process

You can move out of feeling like a victim and dumping anger on others—and into taking personal responsibility for your feelings—with the Anger Process. The Anger Process is a powerful way to release anger that may be in the way of being open to learning. This moves you out of victim-mode and into openheartedness. It results in awareness of what you are doing that your inner child is angry at *you* about. Find a safe and quiet place to do this three-part exercise (the description below imagines that this place is a bedroom, since a bed is a good, safe place on which to do this exercise).

Imagine that the person you are angry at is sitting in front of you. Let your inner child yell, saying in detail everything you wish you could say. Unleash your anger, pain, and resentment until you have nothing more to say. You can scream and cry, pound a pillow, or roll up a towel and beat the bed. (The reason you don't tell the person directly is because this kind of cathartic, no-holds-barred "anger dump" would be abusive.) You can do this out loud or, if you are not comfortable expressing yourself this way or you don't have the privacy to do this, you can do it in writing. What does your inner child want to say to this person or to a situation?

_____

_____

_____

_____

_____

_____

Now ask yourself who this person reminds you of in your past—your mother or father, a grandparent, a sibling? (Note that it may be the same person. That is, you may be mad at your father now, and he is acting just like he did when you were growing up.) Now let your inner child yell at the person from the past thoroughly and energetically—out loud or in writing.

_____

_____

_____

_____

_____

_____

Finally, come back into the present and let your inner child do the same thing with you. Allow your inner child to express anger, pain, and resentment toward you for your part in the situation or for treating yourself the way the people in parts 1 and 2 of the exercise treated you. This brings the problem home to personal responsibility, opening the door to exploring your own behavior. Again, do it out loud or in writing.

_____

_____

_____

_____

_____

_____

After doing an Anger Process, Amy told me the following:

It amazes me to see how the very things that I am angry at my critical mother for are, in fact, the very ways I, in turn, continually parent my inner child. The abuse I have put my inner child through is unbelievable. No wonder I am so anxious. If I were to have parented my physical children in the same manner as I have my inner child, I believe that I may have been charged with child neglect and child abuse. I feel so much regret and remorse for doing this to the sweet, compassionate little girl who is me!

In the last chapter, I introduced you to spiritual bypassing, in which people use spiritual practices, beliefs, or ideals to avoid their feelings. If you tend to do this when you allow your inner child to express anger toward the wounded self for ignoring feelings, the anger might really burst forth. An inner child can feel furious at you for not allowing them to feel, because it leaves them abandoned, discounted, unheard, and unseen, as Arthur discovered.

Arthur was addicted to anger, as well as to self-judgment. Given that he is a priest and wants to be a role model for loving actions, he was deeply disturbed by his angry outbursts. Once he discovered that these current addictions came into his life through his past relationship with his angry and judging father, he could heal and learn. He could handle the painful feeling of helplessness in the face of someone's mean actions or words and also in the face of things not going his way. He is now less afraid of giving his opinion and can accept opinions that differ from his without feeling judged or unaccepted and without getting angry. Mistakes have now become a learning experience for Arthur, rather than something to get angry about.

As you develop your loving adult, you may find that you no longer take others' behavior personally, even when someone is angry or disapproving. When you learn to take responsibility for your own feelings, you stop blaming others for your painful feelings. You begin to realize that your source of worth comes through connection with your Divine guidance, so you are no longer so reactive to others' disapproval.

Other Bridges to Learning

It's often not easy to move out of the intent to control and avoid and into the intent to learn about loving yourself. In addition to the Anger Process, tune in to what else helps you relax and open your heart. For example, does walking in nature, listening to soothing music, hugging a pet, talking with a friend, attending a 12-step meeting, dancing, or doing something creative move you from a closed place to an open place?

Write down all the things you can think of that open your heart to learning when you are stuck in your wounded self.

_____   _____

_____   _____

_____   _____

_____   _____

It takes time and practice to move from a closed heart to an open heart. The quicker you stop yourself from winding down into the darkness of your wounded self, the easier you will find moving into an intent to learn. If you ever get really stuck in a closed place, do the Anger Process.

Becoming a loving adult involves two choices:

- choosing the intent to learn

- choosing to connect with your Divine guidance

We cannot operate as a loving adult until we are connected with our higher guidance.

Beginning to Connect with Your Divine Guidance

Remember, there is no one right form of Divine guidance. Each of us needs to discover what feels right to us and what works for us. Many people have experienced spiritual abuse, meaning that you may have been taught that God is a judgmental man in the sky who dishes out rewards and punishments. Even if you weren't taught this, you might have absorbed it from our society's myths. When this is the case, it's helpful to let go of that concept of God and imagine an unconditionally loving being who is always here for you personally. The following visualization will help you connect with this presence. An audio recording of this visualization is available at http://www.newharbinger.com/43188.

Sit somewhere comfortable, preferably out in nature, if that is possible. Take a few mindful breaths, breathing in relaxation and breathing out tension. Open to your imagination. As William Blake said, "Imagination is Evidence of the Divine." Using your imagination is part of being able to connect with your Divine guidance.

Imagine yourself in a beautiful place in nature. It may be the ocean, the mountains, a forest, or the desert. It may be a meadow. Perhaps there is a waterfall or a brook. Imagine that you can feel the temperature of the air on your skin, hear the sounds of the birds or the water or the wind, smell the flowers or the trees or the salt or the purity of the air, and even taste the air. Use all of your senses as you imagine your beautiful place.

Within this place, become aware of a warm, loving, powerful presence. Your Divine guidance wants to come in whatever form is comfortable for you, so you have an opportunity to imagine exactly how you want your guidance to appear. This presence could be located within you, all around you—or both within you and surrounding you—or it could be seated next to you, like a friend. It could be Jesus, Buddha, Allah, Mother Mary, one of the saints, or an archangel. It could be someone you have known and loved who has died. It could be the highest, wisest, most glorious part of yourself, your own higher self. Or it could take a less specific form—an *inner mentor, a spirit guide, a guardian angel, a teacher. It could also be your experience of nature. It could be a pure light or pure energy or the pure essence of love, compassion, softness, power, strength, and wisdom. It could be something or someone you see or just something you feel. If it is a being other than your higher self or someone you know or know of, you can make up a name for it—whatever name you like, or you can just call it "my guidance." Just use your imagination and open to whatever feels totally safe, loving, wise, and powerful to be held by or to feel within you, whatever you will most want to turn to for love and guidance.*

Your guidance is here now, with you. Feel yourself surrounded by love and filled with love. You can relax and rest in the love of your guidance.

Imagine the peace that surrounds you and is within you as you are with this energy of love. Imagine that your guidance knows everything about you and loves you unconditionally. Imagine that your guidance never leaves you, is always with you and within you. Be with your personal Divine guidance, knowing you can always turn to it for love, wisdom, strength, and truth.

Take some deep breaths and come back into the present.

Describe this being in as much detail as you can, including its name.

_____

_____

_____

_____

_____

_____

_____

With access to Divine guidance, we have a resource we can turn to who will model ways of being and living that are more supportive and helpful than the ways we may have learned from parents and other authority figures. Your guidance is the key to developing your loving adult self.

Beginning to Develop Your Loving Adult Self

Do you have some ideas for how you wish your parents or other caregivers had been with you? Whatever you wanted from your parents or other caregivers is what your inner child now wants from you as a loving adult. And whatever you are now wanting from others—friends, parents, a partner—is also some of what your inner child needs and wants from you.

Write a letter from your inner child to a current person in your life—or an imaginary future partner—telling them what you want and need from them to feel seen, valued, and loved. Take some time to tune in to what it is that makes you feel loved by someone.

_____

_____

_____

_____

_____

Read over what you just wrote, and other than needs that can be met only in a relationship, such as physical affection, lovemaking, companionship, shared laughter, someone having your back, and so on, let your inner child tell you what he or she wants from you, such as being seen, valued, listened to, stood up for, and so on.

_____

_____

_____

_____

_____

Now again, take some mindful breaths, focus in your heart, imagine your Divine guidance, and ask, "What do you want to tell me about being a loving adult with my inner child?" Then let go, as best as you can, and allow the answer to come *through* you, not *from* you. The thoughts of the wounded self come *from* your mind, while the thoughts of your higher guidance come *through* your mind. They may come as words popping into your mind, or the information may come as images or feelings. Don't worry about whether they are accurate or complete. Just write whatever these words, images, or feelings are.

_____

_____

_____

_____

_____

_____

Learning to open ever more deeply to your Divine guidance is unending and ongoing, as we can always learn new ways of being, physically and mentally. Just as your wounded self is strengthened by junk foods and junk thoughts, access to your Divine guidance is strengthened evermore by healthy eating and beneficial thoughts. Making these changes will heighten your frequency and connect you with the energetic vibrations of love, wisdom, and truth.

Eating to Raise Your Frequency

Research from the last ten years shows that 80 percent of our immune system is in our gut. Our gut contains trillions of bacteria—some vital to health and some detrimental. When the good bacteria outweigh the bad bacteria, we generally have good health and a strong immune system. But when the bad bacteria outweigh the good, causing an imbalance called "gut dysbiosis," our immunity is compromised and our health may deteriorate. Gut dysbiosis causes toxicity in the gut that can create "leaky gut syndrome"—holes in the lining of the intestine that allow the toxicity to leach into the blood and then in to other organs, eventually causing illness. In addition, there is a gut-brain axis; when the gut is toxic, the toxicity may go up the vagus nerve into the brain, causing anxiety, depression, and many other brain disorders. For more on this, see the Resources section at the end of this book.

So the connection between gut and brain is clear, as is the connection between gut and body. With this information, it's not hard to understand that a toxic gut lowers our frequency, making it difficult to access our Divine guidance. People often talk about having "gut feelings," and there is a lot to this experience of intuition and guidance. But when our gut is toxic, we may lose access to our gut feelings—our inner source of guidance.

When I ask my clients about their diet, most say that they eat a healthy diet. But when I ask for details, it's evident that this often isn't the case. Richard's story illustrates this.

Richard called me because he had no energy, was depressed, and had become a couch potato, spending most of his time in front of a television. In his mid-sixties, he had no motivation to run his business, though it was successful. He believed in God, but he had no sense of Spirit within him or around him and had no personal communication with his Divine guidance. Overall, he liked his work, was in a happy marriage, and his children were doing well. There was nothing challenging in his life that would account for how he was feeling. I then asked him about his diet and his answer was typical: "I eat a healthy diet." But as I got the details, it was evident to me that his gut was likely out of balance due to his standard American diet. Fortunately, he was open to my suggestions regarding organic foods and some fermented foods. I stressed that if the fermented foods didn't agree with him, he likely had a deeper problem and would need to see a functional medicine doctor.

We then had a few sessions, spread over a couple of months, exploring some false beliefs that also were causing him problems. In his fourth session, he told me that he was feeling great. His energy was back, he was not depressed, he was motivated to do more than he had been doing in his business, he had been getting together with friends to play golf, he and his son were starting a new business together, he was watching hardly any television, and he was able to have two-way conversations with his Divine guidance! He said he had been following my food suggestions and that he was excited with this huge change.

Being very honest with yourself, write down everything you eat, drink, or consume in a day, and whether or not it's organic.

- Breakfast

  _____

  _____

- Lunch

  _____

  _____

- Dinner

  _____

  _____

- Snacks

  _____

  _____

- Beverages, including alcohol and coffee

  _____

  _____

- Over-the-counter drugs, prescription medications, and recreational drugs

  _____

  _____

Recent Changes in How Food Is Produced

There have been many changes in the way food is grown or manufactured over the past two hundred years. Before the rise of factory farms, eggs came from healthy chickens roaming free, gathering nutrients from a wide variety of insects, seeds, and plants on the fertile ground; animals ate their natural foods, and they were not systematically treated cruelly. Today, most meats and eggs are factory farmed; the animals are given hormones, antibiotics, food sprayed with pesticides and laced with GMOs, and foods that aren't natural to their diet. These toxic meats lower your frequency.

Similarly, before the mid-1800s, grain was harvested after it had sprouted. Now it is harvested before it has sprouted, which makes it hard to digest, due to the grain covering, which contains phytic acid, and due to the lectins—all of which protect the grain against destructive insects but also protect against humans being able to fully access its nutrients. Soaking and sprouting generally take care of these issues.

Previously, clean raw milk and other dairy products came from healthy cows or goats. The pasteurized dairy products we have today from factory-farmed cows cause many health problems, and they lower your frequency.

Highly processed sugar and processed carbs—including altered wheat with its "super gluten"—which turn into sugar in the body, were not available at all. But today they are everywhere in the packaged non-foods and sodas on supermarket shelves and are greatly responsible for the rampant obesity in our society.

In addition to junk foods causing a gut imbalance, drugs also contribute to the harmful bacteria. Antibiotics destroy both good and bad bacteria, leaving the gut vulnerable to an even greater imbalance, unless it is replenished with pre- and probiotics from organic vegetables and organic fermented foods. Do some research online regarding what creates a healthy microbiome—a healthy gut. Educate yourself regarding what foods are nutrient dense and contribute to health, and which of the foods you are eating are harming your health and lowering your frequency.

Whether you are paleo, keto, vegetarian, or vegan—or none of those—the important thing about food and your frequency is that you eat fresh, organic, and unprocessed foods, and foods that grow from nature and have not been genetically tampered with, as much as possible.

Depending on your diet preferences, here are the foods I recommend you choose from:

- Lots of organic fruits and vegetables, sprouts.

- Organic, sprouted seeds and nuts.

- Soaked beans and whole grains such as quinoa, millet, and ancient grains. Be sure to stay away from wheat. Be careful about beans and grains, because if you have gut dysbiosis, the bad bacteria may be feeding off them, as they thrive on some forms of carbohydrates.

- Healthy fats, such as coconut oil, olive oil, and medium-chain triglyceride (MCT), and the fats found in olives, avocados, ground flax seeds, sprouted seeds and nuts, and nut butters. Also, if you eat dairy and eggs, organic butter and ghee and eggs from organically raised, pastured hens. If you eat meat, lard and tallow from grass-fed animals, as well as the fat within the meat. (Remember, the fat from factory-farmed animals is toxic, but not the fat from grass-fed animals.)

- Some fermented foods with each meal—olives, sauerkraut and other fermented vegetables, kombucha, and fermented soy products such as miso, natto, and tempeh (unfermented soy may cause digestive problems and contains phytates that can cause mineral deficiencies in vegetarians and vegans, as well as goitrogens, which can impact your thyroid function, and phytoestrogens, which can mimic and even block estrogen). Also, if you eat dairy, plain organic yogurt and kefir from grass-fed dairy animals. (If you have problems with the fermented foods, this indicates that there might be a deeper issue, perhaps a problem called "small intestinal bacterial overgrowth" [SIBO], and you will need to work with a functional medicine doctor to discover the root cause and heal it.)

- If you eat dairy products, make sure they come from organic, grass-fed cows, goats, or sheep.

- If you eat fish, be sure it is wild-caught fish.

- If you eat eggs, make sure they are from organically raised, pastured hens.

- If you eat meat, bone broth and moderate amounts of organically raised, grass-fed meats and pastured poultry.

Special considerations must be taken into account for vegetarians, vegans, and those meat-eaters who are interested in lowering the amount of meat and dairy in their diet (or eliminating it entirely):

- Iron is plentiful in vegetables, beans, lentils, whole grains, and seaweed.

- Calcium is available in large quantities of organic dark leafy greens.

- Vitamin B12 comes primarily from animal sources, so you need to take a vitamin supplement, perhaps along with some seaweed.

- Omega-3 fatty acids can be obtained from organic sprouted seeds and nuts.

Try eliminating grains and dairy for a month to see how you feel. Even if you are lacto-intolerant, you might do well on plain organic yogurt and kefir from grass-fed cows.

If you are ill, see a functional medicine doctor to get at the root cause of the problem and begin a healing protocol. Conventional medicine is great for broken bones and necessary surgery, but it is sorely lacking in dealing with chronic illness and fatigue. Functional medicine deals with the root causes of illness and offers a healing protocol, while conventional medicine deals with symptoms and generally prescribes drugs for the symptoms, often causing unwanted side effects and even more gut problems.

Looking over the list you made of the foods, beverages, and drugs you currently consume, decide what you will begin to change now.

The diet changes I will make right now are:

_____

_____

_____

_____

You might want to keep a food journal, writing down everything you consume and how you feel right after, a few hours after, a day after, and a few days after eating. You need to start to connect some of your physical and emotional feelings with the food you eat. This will deepen your awareness of changes regarding your energy, general health, ability to focus, and your ability to connect with your Divine guidance.

Learn More About Your Thought Frequency

If your intent in opening to your Divine guidance is anything other than to continue to evolve as a loving person, your wounded self is attached to an outcome, which means that your intent is to control rather than to learn about loving yourself. This will keep your frequency too low to access your Divine guidance. The wounded self can be tricky when it comes to intent. It can mask itself as a loving adult and even as your Divine guidance, creating much confusion. Consider what your actual agenda might be when you believe you are opening to learning.

When I think I'm opening to learning with my Divine guidance, but I'm not focused on becoming a more loving person, my real agenda is:

_____   I'm hoping to get love

_____   I'm hoping to increase my income

_____   I want to lose weight

_____   I'm hoping to find the love of my life

_____   I'm hoping to discover my passion and purpose

_____   Other: _____

_____   Other: _____

While there is no problem with having any of these goals, if you are attaching your worth and happiness to achieving a particular outcome, your wounded self is in charge with an intent to control, and your frequency won't be high enough to access your Divine guidance. All forms of control and any form of self-abandonment—judging yourself, staying in your mind rather than being present in your body, turning to various addictions to numb your feelings, and making others and outcomes responsible for your feelings—will keep your frequency too low to access your Divine guidance.

The only intent that raises your frequency high enough to access your Divine guidance is the intent to learn about loving yourself and others—to be on the soul's journey of evolving in your ability to love and desiring to manifest love with others and the planet. What might be in the way of your embracing your soul's journey of love? What is more important to you than being on your true soul's journey?

Again, being honest with yourself, go within, and write what comes to you when you ask yourself this question: "What's more important to me than being loving to myself, others, and the planet?"

_____

_____

_____

_____

The reason step 1 is about becoming aware of your feelings is because it's easier to notice your feelings than it is to be aware of your intent and resulting thoughts. We become empowered when we are able to connect our feelings with our own choices. See if you can start to become aware of these connections by identifying what you tell yourself with your feelings. Remember, however, that anxiety and depression can come from toxicity in your brain due to toxicity in your gut, as well as from dissociated or unhealed childhood abuse.

When I feel *anxious*, what I'm telling myself or how I'm treating myself from my wounded self, with the intent to control, is:

_____

_____

_____

When I feel *depressed*, what I'm telling myself or how I'm treating myself from my wounded self, with the intent to control, is:

_____

_____

_____

When I feel *guilty*, what I'm telling myself or how I'm treating myself from my wounded self, with the intent to control, is:

_____

_____

_____

When I feel *shame*, what I'm telling myself or how I'm treating myself from my wounded self, with the intent to control, is:

_____

_____

_____

When I feel *angry*, what I'm telling myself or how I'm treating myself from my wounded self, with the intent to control, is:

_____

_____

_____

When I feel *empty* or *alone*, what I'm telling myself or how I'm treating myself from my wounded self, with the intent to control, is:

_____

_____

_____

When I feel *jealous*, what I'm telling myself or how I'm treating myself from my wounded self, with the intent to control, is:

_____

_____

_____

When my *feelings are hurt*, what I'm telling myself or how I'm treating myself from my wounded self, with the intent to control, is:

_____

_____

_____

When I feel *peaceful*, what I'm telling myself or how I'm treating myself from my loving adult, with the intent to learn, is:

_____

_____

_____

When I feel *joyful*, what I'm telling myself or how I'm treating myself from my loving adult, with the intent to learn, is:

_____

_____

_____

When I feel *full of love inside*, what I'm telling myself or how I'm treating myself from my loving adult, with the intent to learn, is:

_____

_____

_____

When I feel *energized* and *alive*, what I'm telling myself or how I'm treating myself from my loving adult, with the intent to learn, is:

_____

_____

_____

You need to accept that as long as you are keeping your frequency too low with junk food and junk thoughts and with controlling, avoidant behavior, you will likely not be able to achieve at-will Divine connection. It's all about your intent and the resulting frequency.

It's the responsibility of your loving adult to keep your frequency high enough to access your Divine guidance by practicing choosing the intent to learn about what is loving to you, moment by moment. We will be going deeper into this as we continue through the rest of the steps of Inner Bonding.

Summing Up the Different Parts of Us

It's important to understand the differences between the wounded self, the inner child, the loving adult, and Divine guidance.

- The *wounded self* is a programmed, conditioned thought process located in the lower brain. Because its intention is always to control, it is incapable of Divine connection and therefore has no access to truth. It operates from fear and false beliefs, and it often makes things up that have nothing to do with reality.

- The *inner child* is a feeling process located in the body and is an individualized expression of the Divine. The inner child often reflects Divine truth through feelings and inner knowing or intuition.

- The *loving adult* is located in the heart, is connected with the love, wisdom, and truth of Divine guidance, and is capable of taking loving action on behalf of self and others.

- *Divine guidance* is spirit and is love, wisdom, truth, peace, and joy. It is the creative force of the universe and is within each of us and all around us.

Inner Dialoguing with Your Inner Child and Your Wounded Self

Only when the subconscious or unconscious false beliefs that have limited you for so long are understood and identified can they be replaced by new and healthy truths that will nurture and heal you. In this step, with the kindness, gentleness, and compassion toward yourself of the loving adult, you will

- explore what you are telling yourself and how you are treating yourself that is causing the wounded feelings,

- discover the programmed thoughts and false beliefs from your wounded self that have led to the self-abandonment that is causing your current shame, fear, anxiety, depression, and other wounded pain,

- look at what may be happening with a person or event that is causing the existential painful feelings of loneliness, heartache, heartbreak, helplessness, or grief, and learn how to release and learn from this pain of life, and

- get to know your true self—your essence, your inner child, your feeling self—and discover what brings you joy.

It's easier to stay focused if you do the dialogue processes in this step out loud or in writing, especially when you are first learning Inner Bonding. With time and practice, you can eventually do it silently in your mind. However, even after many years of practicing Inner Bonding, I still do it out loud every morning on my walk in nature, and if I get stuck with something, I do it in writing.

False Beliefs of the Wounded Self

Before learning to dialogue, let's deepen the understanding of your wounded self and your true soul self. Our wounded self is the aspect of us that has been programmed with many fears and false beliefs. While it helped us survive as children, it is now the main obstacle preventing us from experiencing Divine connection. When our intent is to control our feelings, as well as control others and outcomes, we are operating from our wounded self.

Our wounded self can be different ages in different situations. If you learned to judge yourself when you were six, you may be operating from a six-year-old aspect of yourself when you are judging yourself. If you discovered at ten years old that food filled you and took away some of the pain, it's likely that your ten-year-old wounded self is in charge if you are binging or eating junk.

Growing up, we all absorbed false beliefs that cause us to abandon ourselves. You might find yourself doing various forms of self-abandonment at different times. Whenever we are abandoning ourselves, we feel rejected, and then we may believe that it is others who are rejecting us, rather than understanding that it is we who are rejecting ourselves.

False beliefs also limit your frequency and, therefore, your ability to connect with your Divine guidance. Often these beliefs are background noise—subconscious junk thoughts that create your wounded feelings. Becoming aware of your limiting, false beliefs and learning to access the truth is vital for raising your frequency and being able to access your Divine guidance. I invite you to begin the process of doing this now.

Breathe into your body, scanning your body for the physical sensations that let you know you are feeling wounded, such as anxiety, depression, guilt, shame, anger, despair, aloneness, emptiness, or hopelessness. If you don't currently have a wounded feeling, remember the last time you felt one or more of these feelings and get present inside your body, imagining those feelings.

Ask yourself, "What am I telling myself, and how am I treating myself? What am I doing or not doing that is self-abandoning and that is causing this feeling?"

Go inside and be honest with yourself as you go through the following ways you might abandon yourself. Again, please be gentle with yourself. Your wounded self needs kindness, not judgment.

Do you stay focused in your head while ignoring your feelings? Do you allow your wounded self to ruminate about all you have to do, to list all the things that are wrong with you, or to analyze yourself? Do you stay focused on what others are doing, analyzing them instead of attending to your own feelings?

_____

_____

Do you turn to various addictions—substances, activities, and controlling behaviors—to avoid feeling your feelings?

_____

_____

Do you make others responsible for your feelings and then try to have control over getting them to give you the love, attention, approval, and validation that you are not giving to yourself?

_____

_____

Are you judging yourself? If you are, what is the judgment? Are you telling yourself that you are not good enough, that you are inadequate or a loser, or that you are unlovable, unimportant, or flawed?

_____

_____

_____

_____

_____

Are you pressuring yourself? If you are, what are you saying? Are you telling yourself that you have to do everything right, that you have to be perfect? Or are you telling yourself that you are okay only if others like you and approve of you, and you can control how they feel about you by being perfect?

_____

_____

_____

_____

_____

What else are you telling yourself, and how else are you abandoning yourself—what you are doing or not doing—that is causing anxiety (or depression, guilt, shame, anger, despair, aloneness, emptiness, or hopelessness)?

_____

_____

_____

_____

_____

_____

Begin to connect your wounded feelings with the self-abandoning junk thoughts and resulting actions from your wounded self. These junk thoughts are the beliefs and myths you absorbed a long time ago from parents, siblings, friends, teachers, and the media that are causing your frequency to be too low to access your Divine guidance.

Again, if you are not aware of what you are telling yourself and how you are treating yourself, no worries. Tuning in to your false beliefs is a process, not an event. Right now, it's just important to start to become aware that when you are unable to connect with your Divine guidance, it might be because of the false beliefs—the junk thoughts—of your wounded self.

The Wounded Self Is Authoritarian or Permissive

If you had a parent who was authoritarian or permissive, you might have incorporated these ways of treating yourself from your wounded self. We are authoritarian when we set rigid limits or expectations on what we can and can't do or what we should do, such as consistently over-exercising or never being able to have dessert or spend money to have fun, even if money isn't a problem. We are being permissive when we indulge in behaviors that are not in our highest good, such as drinking too much, eating junk, or taking our anger out on others by being emotionally or physically abusive. Much of the pain in our culture is from people who are acting from their authoritarian and permissive wounded selves.

Being honest with yourself, without judgment, ask yourself what are the ways in which you set rigid limits on yourself that are not necessarily in your highest good?

_____

_____

_____

_____

Again, being honest with yourself, without judgment, ask yourself what are the ways you are indulging in behaviors that are not in your highest good or in the highest good of others—perhaps justifying them by telling yourself you are actually being loving to yourself?

_____

_____

_____

_____

The wounded self likes to stay hidden—it doesn't want to be unmasked, because if it were, it would lose control over you. And because this wounded part of us hides itself, it takes time to peel away the layers of false beliefs. Even after all these years of practicing Inner Bonding, I still occasionally uncover a false belief. I love it when I come upon a hidden false belief, because then I can open to learning with my Divine guidance about the truth and take loving actions based on the truth, rather than continuing to operate from a belief that isn't serving me well.

The Purpose of Shame

Have you struggled with shame? The feelings of shame come from the false belief that there is something basically wrong with you—that you are somehow flawed, defective, not good enough, bad, or inadequate. I suffered from painful shame for years, and then I discovered two choices that enabled me to completely heal my shame.

- I learned to define my worth by my intrinsic soul qualities, rather than placing my worth on externals, such as looks and performance.

- I discovered that shaming myself was a *form of control*. As long as my wounded self believed that others' unloving and rejecting behavior toward me was my fault, because I wasn't good enough, I could continue to believe that if only I changed, I could control their behavior toward me. Magically, when I finally fully accepted my lack of control over others' feelings and behavior, my shame disappeared and has never returned.

I had spent years in therapy trying to heal my shame, but it wasn't until I addressed these two issues that my shame was healed. You can explore this yourself.

> When someone rejects you, gets angry at you, blames you, withdraws from you, resists you, or in any other way is unloving to you, what do you tell yourself? See if you can tune in to the wounded part of you that might be telling you that it's your fault. What do you tell yourself that makes this person's behavior your fault?
>
> _____
>
> _____
>
> _____

While others may often reflect back to you how you are treating yourself, you don't control how others choose to react, so you are not the cause of their rejecting, angry, withdrawn, or blaming wounded behavior. For example, if you are invisible to yourself, not seeing, valuing, or listening to yourself, you might end up feeling invisible to others. They might not see, value, or listen to you when you are abandoning yourself, but this is different than their wounded, controlling behavior of anger, blame, or withdrawal. You don't control how they choose to respond to you.

What they are reacting to is your wounded self, *not* your beautiful essence. And unfortunately, they might be reacting to your wounded self with their own wounded self, which you have no control over.

You have control over your own intent and whether you are operating from your wounded self or your loving adult, but you have no control over their intent and whether they are operating from their judgmental wounded self or their accepting loving adult.

> If you deeply valued your beautiful essence and you fully accepted your lack of control over others, would you continue to blame and shame yourself? How would you treat yourself if you valued yourself and accepted your helplessness over others' intent?
>
> _____
>
> _____
>
> _____
>
> _____

You will be amazed at how quickly shame heals when you learn to see and value your beautiful essence—which you will learn to do in this workbook—and when you fully accept your lack of control over others' intention and resulting behavior.

Kurt was raised by a single mother who had no time for him and who blamed him for her situation in life. Kurt's father disappeared soon after he was born, and his mother had to drop out of school and go to work to support herself and Kurt. Not surprisingly, Kurt learned to judge himself when others were upset with him or disconnected from him, resulting in deep feelings of shame. He said to me, "Shame has been the hardest and most difficult feeling for me to work with, especially when I am stuck in a state of helplessness over someone blaming me or disconnecting from me."

Kurt's brain had spent a long time wired to go automatically into shame, but now, being in shame felt so bad to him that he became motivated both to explore what happened to cause it and to move out of his wounded self to learn about who he truly was. "I've learned that the shame came from the need to judge and blame myself for my mother's unloving behavior toward me. I needed to tell myself that it was my fault, because there was something wrong with me, and that was why she was disconnecting from me and treating me in an uncaring way, rather than accept my helplessness over her. I think I would have died as a child if I had accepted that there was nothing I could do about how *my mother treated me. Also, I unconsciously internalized much of what my mother told me was wrong with me."*

Kurt is now able to come into the truth about how painful and sad his childhood was. What seemed like an extremely difficult feeling to let go of is finally lifting and dissipating into truth and love toward himself.

No matter what you experienced as a child, you can learn to treat yourself with love and kindness and heal the shame that limits you.

The Fear of Death

The fear of death often keeps people from fully living their life. Protecting yourself against death lowers your frequency, while fully living your life to creatively express your passion and purpose raises your frequency and enables you to connect with your Divine guidance. One cause of the fear of death is the false belief that you are your body and that when your body dies, you die.

It is the wounded self who identifies with the body and therefore fears death. When you have access to your spiritual source of truth, you will know that your soul is immortal, that your Divine guidance is unconditionally loving, and that there is never any punishment or hell. When you know these things, you lose your fear of death, and you let go of all the ways you hold yourself back to protect against death.

What are your beliefs about what happens when you die?

_____

_____

_____

How do your beliefs make you feel about death?

_____

_____

How are you currently limiting yourself because of your fear of death? What would you be doing that you are currently not doing if you weren't afraid of death?

_____

_____

_____

Remember, beliefs that scare you are lies coming from your wounded self. The truth makes you feel safe and free. If you have a fear of death, you might want to read some of the more recent books about near death experiences, such as *Dying To Be Me: My Journey from Cancer, to Near Death, to True Healing,* by Anita Moorjani (Carlsbad, CA: Hay House, 2012), and *Proof of Heaven: A Neurosurgeon's Journey into the Afterlife,* by Eben Alexander, MD (New York: Simon and Schuster, 2012).

Discovering Sources of Your False Beliefs

The following exercise is designed to help you remember events and situations from your childhood. It will lay the groundwork for pinpointing your false beliefs.

Take some deep, mindful breaths, getting present in your body, relaxing your feet … your legs … your pelvis … your back … your chest … your shoulders … your arms … your neck … your face … your ears … your scalp … bringing in relaxation with every inhale and releasing tension with every exhale.

Now let yourself go back in time to when you were a child, remembering your house, your room, your family, or remembering not having a family or a house—living with foster parents, in an orphanage, or on the streets. Go through the list of questions below and write what is true for you. If you want to write down the memories that arise in response, or any images or messages you recall, have another sheet of paper available.

Do you think your parents or caregivers liked you?

_____

Did they think you were a wonderful person, or did they often say or imply that was there something wrong with you?

_____

Did you often feel that you were just not good enough?

_____

Did you believe you were a bad person? _____

If you lived with your parents, how did they treat each other?

- Open and respectful? _____

- One angry and the other compliant or resistant? _____

- Both angry? _____

- Ignoring each other? _____

- Shaming and blaming each other? _____

- Nagging? _____

- Was there violence in your home? _____

How did your parents or other caregivers treat themselves?

- Did they abuse substances? Alcohol, drugs, food?

  _____

  _____

- Did one always put himself or herself aside for the other?

  _____

- Did either of your parents or caregivers allow himself or herself to be physically, sexually, or emotionally abused?

  _____

- Were one or both always overworked? _____

- Did either of them ever play?

  _____

- Did either of them ask for what they wanted?

  _____

- Did either of them take responsibility for their own happiness?

  _____

- Were either of them happy some of the time? Much of the time?

  _____

- Was there ever joy in your home?

  _____

How did your parents or caregivers deal with pain?

- Did they see it as weak to show pain? _____

- Did you ever see either of them cry? _____

- Were they victims, or did they take responsibility for their pain?

  _____

- Were they there for each other when one was in pain?

  _____

- Were they there for you when you were in pain?

  _____

- Was anyone ever there for your pain?

  _____

- Did you get the message that they couldn't handle their own pain or yours?

  _____

- Did they shame you for your pain and your tears?

  _____

How did your parents or other caregivers treat you when they were needy, lonely, angry, anxious, overwhelmed, or drunk? Did they yell at you, beat you, sexually abuse you, neglect or ignore you, smother you, shame you, threaten you, blame you, or nag at you?

_____

_____

Remember a time when you did something your parents or other caregivers didn't like—you broke a toy or broke something of theirs, did poorly in school, talked back, cried, hit a sibling or another child, or got into some other sort of trouble. How did they handle it? Were they angry, violent, disapproving, hard, silent, critical, judgmental, shaming, cold, nagging, and so on, or were they loving, understanding, caring, and open?

_____

_____

How did you feel if they were unloving to you? _____

If you remember feeling sad, alone, lonely, scared, hurt, trapped, or abused, remember what was happening at that time. See if you can remember what conclusions about your worth or about Spirit or about other people you drew from that situation or those situations.

_____

_____

_____

_____

If you had siblings, how did you get along with them?

_____

_____

- Did you have a sibling who was mean to you?

    _____

- Did your parents or caregivers protect you from being harmed by your sibling, or did they ignore the situation?

    _____

- Did they trust your account, or did they disbelieve you?

    _____

- Were you the one who was mean, and your parents ignored that too?

    _____

When you did something positive—accomplished something, got good grades, were kind to someone, or demonstrated your talents—how did they respond to you?

_____

Were they interested and loving, or did they ignore you?

_____

Did they attend important school events, or were they too busy or uninterested?

_____

Did you feel important or unimportant to them?

_____

Did you ever feel like you were a bother or a burden?

_____

Write whatever conclusions you are currently aware of that you drew from the family experiences you marked.

_____

_____

_____

_____

_____

Discovering How You Treat Your Inner Child

Take some deep breaths, or take a walk or a break. When you are ready, allow yourself to become aware of how you treat your inner child.

Let your awareness go inward and see what you, as your wounded self, do when you are feeling angry or hurt or scared or alone or in grief. Is your wounded self like one or both of your parents or other caregivers?

_____

_____

_____

How do you handle your difficult or painful feelings?

Do you eat, take medication, drink, or use drugs?

_____

Do you get angry and blame others for your feelings?

_____

Do you ignore your feelings until they make you sick?

_____

Do you engage in some activity such as work, sex, or watching television, hoping to blot them out?

_____

Do you discount them as being silly or over-reactive?

_____

Do you criticize yourself for having these feelings, telling yourself that there is something wrong with you for your feelings?

_____

Do you run away, ignoring your feelings?

_____

Do you shut down, withdraw, or go numb—resisting feeling your feelings?

_____

Do you try to plug into others, hoping to get them to caretake your feelings?

_____

Do you caretake others' difficult or painful feelings while ignoring your own?

_____

Write whatever conclusions you are currently aware of that you drew from the family experiences you marked above that are related to how you treat your inner child.

_____

_____

_____

_____

_____

_____

Discovering How Your Inner Child Feels

Now take another break, and when you are ready, allow yourself to feel the child within you. Move inside your body and feel what it is like to be alone with no loving adult there to love and care for you.

How do you, as the inner child, feel when your wounded self ignores, criticizes, discounts, runs away from, shuts down, or blots out your feelings?

_____

_____

_____

_____

_____

How do you feel when your wounded self is shaming or indulgent?

_____

_____

Do you feel alone, sad, anxious, unimportant, angry, depressed, numb, victimized, scared, or overwhelmed?

_____

Now move into your loving adult, breathing into your heart, and see your wounded self and your inner child—compassionately embracing all aspects of yourself.

Write whatever other conclusions you are currently aware of that you drew from these experiences:

_____

_____

_____

_____

The Wounded Self Tries to Control Others

We all learned many ways to attempt to get love, approval, and attention or to avoid disapproval, rejection, or engulfment. Again, while you needed these survival mechanisms as you were growing up, they are now lowering your frequency and may be causing major relationship problems.

As you read about the various ways you might have learned to try to control others, again be caring, compassionate, and gentle with yourself. If you judge yourself, you will cut off your learning and healing, and self-judgment keeps your frequency too low to access your Divine guidance. So be kind and extend some compassion to yourself.

Do you try to have control over getting what you want from others with anger, blame, interrogating, shame, threats, and similar forms of intimidation?

_____

_____

Are you overly nice, giving, compliant, and people pleasing—giving yourself up—in the hopes others will love you and approve of you, or at least not get angry with you or reject you?

_____

_____

Do you complain, explain, defend, share your feelings as a form of blame, lie, or lecture in an attempt to convince others that you are right?

_____

_____

Are you overly dramatic or use illness as a form of control?

_____

_____

Do you shut down and withdraw your love as a form of punishment, hoping to get others to stop what they are doing that feels unloving to you?

_____

_____

Do you resist giving others what they want, fearing that you will be controlled by them, engulfed and smothered by them, and lose yourself in the relationship?

_____

_____

Go inside and honestly assess what else you do in your relationships to try to have control over getting love and approval, and avoiding rejection and engulfment. What other ways do you use to try to control others?

_____

_____

_____

What generally happens between you and a partner, a parent, a child, or a friend when you try to control your relationship to get love and avoid disapproval or rejection? Do any of these forms of control create a sense of safety between you and the other person? Do they create loving feelings and emotional intimacy? Even if the other person gives in, is the energy between you loving and connected?

_____

_____

_____

_____

The wounded self believes that you can have control over others loving you or not rejecting you, but this is a major false belief. The only thing you actually have control over is whether or not you are loving yourself or you are rejecting and abandoning yourself. And again, any form of controlling behavior lowers your frequency and makes it hard to connect with your Divine guidance.

MaryAnne's father wanted a son, so when MaryAnne was born, he rejected her. She grew up believing that she had to seek her father's approval for her survival. She finally felt some acceptance from him when she did well in school, and she developed the belief that she had to continue to please him all the time or he would reject her again.

Her religion taught her to always put others before herself and to deny her own needs, feelings, and wishes. It's no wonder that MaryAnne learned to completely sacrifice herself to others' wishes, which, of course, included her husband. She even had an abortion, which was against her principles, because that is what he wanted her to do, and she feared being rejected by him. She thought she could control him into loving her if she gave herself up. But instead of loving her, he did what people do who have a fear of being controlled—he resisted her, and their marriage went on the rocks.

It took a while for MaryAnne to discern the difference between loving herself and being selfish and to let go of her false belief that she needed to sacrifice herself to others, but finally she saw that it was her husband who was being selfish in expecting her to abandon herself to please him. She devoted herself to learning to love herself, and she eventually told me that, "My children have benefitted the most from the new me, but I think that all my relationships and even casual encounters are much the better for it."

Wounded Self Triggers

You might find yourself feeling happy and centered, and then suddenly something triggers you into your wounded self, into controlling or avoiding. It's important to become aware of what these triggers are, because the moment you are triggered into your wounded self, your frequency goes down, and you no longer have access to the love and truth of your Divine guidance.

In fact, when we are triggered into our wounded self, we don't even have access to logical thinking. Our logic and reason comes from the higher brain, but our wounded self is in our lower brain, and when we are triggered, and our intent is to control or avoid, we have no access to reason. We are operating from fear and from our old programmed beliefs.

There are many kinds of triggers. Take a moment to contemplate what triggers you.

- someone's anger, disapproval, criticism, judgment, or rejection

- others projecting onto you and blaming you for something they are doing

- feeling misunderstood and unseen by someone

- others being needy and wanting you to fix them, rescue them, validate them, approve of them or fill them up

- a partner pulling on you for sex

- a partner rejecting you for sex

- someone withdrawing and shutting you out

- someone lying to you or betraying you in some way

- situations in which you feel helpless over a person or an event

- others procrastinating, resisting, doing a mediocre job, or being incompetent

- a painful event

- the news and current world events

- people being late

- someone's messiness in your environment

- your own existential painful feelings, such as loneliness or heartbreak

Again, we are all different, so what upsets another person might not be upsetting you.

What often scares you and triggers you into your wounded self with your controlling and avoidant behavior?

_____

_____

_____

_____

_____

In order to connect with your Divine guidance, you will have to shift your intent. Doing these exercises have helped you become more aware of your wounded self so you can learn to consciously choose to shift your intent from controlling to loving. Before I developed my loving adult, anyone's disapproval or anger instantly triggered me into fear, stress, and shame, and I would give myself up, scurrying around to try to please them. The fear, stress, and shame would stay with me for hours and sometimes days—not a fun way to live. Inner peace consistently eluded me.

Once I fully accepted that I have no control over others' intent, and I fully accepted that their behavior is about them—not about me—I was no longer triggered into my wounded self by their unloving behavior. Now I'm compassionately present as a loving adult with the painful feelings of life that I always feel when others are unloving, and I disengage to take loving care of myself. Choosing to love myself rather than abandon myself allows the feelings to pass through me quickly rather than stay stuck in my body, and I'm able to remain peaceful within. My inner child feels safe, knowing that I'm here taking care of my feelings and connecting with my Divine guidance for comfort and wisdom. This can be true for you.

Discovering Projections

The wounded self is often a master of projection. Projection occurs when you deny your own feelings and behavior and instead are attributing them to another person. Common projections are:

- "You're selfish." Translation: I'm being selfish, but I don't want to admit it or deal with it.

- "You're closed." Translation: I'm closed, but I don't want to open or admit that I'm closed.

- "You're judgmental." Translation: I'm judging myself, and I feel ashamed of this, so it's easier to blame you instead.

- "You're angry." Translation: I'm angry, but I judge myself for being angry, so I won't admit it.

- "Everything is about you." Translation: I'm being narcissistic, but I don't want to know this.

- "You're crazy." Translation: I'm feeling or acting out of control, but I can't let myself know this.

- "You're abusive." Translation: I'm being abusive, but I refuse to deal with myself.

- "You don't love me or care about me." Translation: I don't love or care about myself, and I don't want responsibility for myself.

Again, be honest with yourself regarding your projections, without judging yourself for projecting. See if you can tune in to some of your projections.

Some of my projections are:

_____

_____

_____

_____

_____

Once again, please be very kind toward yourself regarding your wounded behaviors. We all have a wounded self, and in order to heal and connect with your Divine guidance, you need to be gentle, caring, and compassionate with yourself, not judgmental. The more you become aware of the fears, false beliefs, and unloving behaviors of the wounded self—with kindness and acceptance—the greater chance you have of keeping your frequency high enough to access your Divine guidance.

Your Inner Child: Your True Soul Self

Your wounded self doesn't know that you are a beautiful and incredible soul—an individual spark of the Divine. When you were not loved in the way you needed, you likely decided that who you are isn't okay, which is when you started to develop your wounded self. Given that your wounded self believes that you are not good enough, you can't see your beautiful soul essence—your inner child—through the eyes of your wounded self. In order to see, value, and truly love who you really are, you need to be able to see yourself through the eyes of your Divine guidance—your source of truth.

Your soul is huge, way too big to fit into your body. You might want to watch Dr. Jill Bolte Taylor's TED talk, "My Stroke of Insight," or read her wonderful book, which has the same title. Taylor, a neuroanatomist, had a devastating stroke at the age of thirty-seven. Her left brain went completely off-line, and her right brain took over, enabling her to leave her body at will. One of the things that astounded her was seeing how huge her soul is, and that only a part of her soul could fit into her body.

The part of our soul that is within us is our true self—our inner child—and the rest of our soul is all around us—our higher self. Here is a visualization that will help you begin to see the beauty of your true, soul self. An audio recording of this visualization is available at http://www.newharbinger.com/43188.

Take some deep breaths and go back to the beautiful place in nature that you visualized in the last chapter, when learning to access your Divine guidance. Imagine that you are smelling the air, hearing the sounds, feeling the temperature on your skin, tasting the air.

While you are in this beautiful place with your guidance, allow yourself to go backward in time to a painful event in childhood or just a time when you were sad and lonely. It may be a time when you felt rejected at home or at school, when you had been abused physically or sexually, when you were alone and neglected, or when you felt shamed or hurt. It may be a time when you were hospitalized and alone. Or, if you have memories of your infancy, it may even be when you were an infant alone in your crib, crying, and no one was coming. Imagine yourself as that infant or child alone in your room, in your crib, on the playground, in the hospital, or outside—lonely and in pain. Let yourself get a clear image of a time when you felt most alone and afraid.

Imagine yourself as you are now, a loving adult, coming into the room or place where you are as an infant or child, along with your Divine guidance. Introduce yourself to yourself as a child, and imagine the wonder in your child's face as he or she recognizes you. Now take your child on your lap and proceed to become the most loving adult you can imagine—holding, stroking, talking, reassuring, and compassionately hearing the child's pain. Or, if the memory is of you as a baby, pick yourself and rock yourself in a rocking chair, bringing Divine Love into yourself as a baby.

Let your inner child know that you are learning to love him or her so that you can always be there for him or her, now that you are grown up. Feel your child relaxing against you with relief that you are there right now.

Now bring your child to the beautiful place in nature. Again, imagine you are sitting and holding your child—smelling the air, hearing the sounds, feeling the temperature on your skin, tasting the air. Now imagine that your guidance is with you, surrounding you and filling you while you are holding your inner child. Imagine love as the color violet, and violet is all around you and within you. Say to yourself, "I am within love, and love is within me. I am within the universe, and the universe is within me."

Now imagine that the love that is within you, the violet that is within you, is your inner child. You can see your inner child—your soul self—through the eyes of your Divine guidance, the eyes of love. Imagine that you can see what your guidance loves about who you really are and that you can see the love that you are. Look into your child's eyes and see who you really are. See your light, your goodness, innocence, vulnerability, aliveness, and lovingness. See your inner child's joy and the special way your child laughs when he or she is happy. See your soul's uniqueness. See how precious your child is, how inherently lovable. See the special gifts you've been given.

See that your child is worthy of being loved and cared for by you. See that this little child just wants to be loved and be loving. See all the different ways he or she behaves when being unloved or feeling afraid of being unloved.

Now imagine that surrounding your true soul self is your wounded self. Imagine seeing your wounded self through the eyes of your guidance. You can see the fear, hurt, shame, and anger—and all the ways your wounded self tries to control. Feel the deep love and compassion your guidance has for your wounded self. Within your wounded self is your true soul essence, but notice that your wounded self does not know that this light and love is within and that it is your responsibility to love both your wounded self and your true soul self, with the help of your guidance, to know who you really are.

Pull your child into you—pulling in all his or her feelings, aliveness, passion, knowingness, sweetness, goodness, vulnerability, pain, fear, anger, and joy. Feel your child within you. You might want to imagine adopting your inner child—agreeing to take responsibility for defining your own worth and taking care of your own feelings. When you feel your child fully owned and within you, open your eyes and come back into the present.

If this child were your actual child, who is exactly like you were before your wounded self took over, and whom you adore, how would you describe this child to someone? What are the gifts you've been given? We all have gifts, and it's often our gifts, such as a gift of sensitivity, curiosity, empathy, or introversion, that have been judged as bad or wrong and therefore suppressed.

Take some time now to see who you really are in your essence, your true self, and write down what you see:

_____

_____

_____

_____

_____

_____

This is the beginning of getting to know, value, and cherish who you really are. The more you are able to see how incredible your soul self is and the gifts you've been given, the easier it will be to be devoted to loving yourself.

Kristen came from a family of boisterous, business-oriented extroverts. Because no one in her family ever valued her sensitivity, sweetness, and quietness, Kristen grew up believing that she wasn't good enough and that she had to figure out a way to be a highly successful extrovert. She constantly judged herself for her business failures and for her quietness, which led to her feeling constant anxiety.

Kristen married a man much like the successful extroverts she grew up with and continued to berate herself for not being more like him. She constantly feared losing him, believing that if he discovered that she was never going to be an outgoing, high-powered businesswoman, he would be disappointed in her and leave her.

As Kristen learned to connect with her spiritual guidance, she gradually saw that her inner child was completely different than the rest of her family, and she began to value her kindness, intuitiveness, and quietness. She finally saw that she loved being there for her husband and children and that this was, in fact, what drew her husband to her. As she took the pressure off herself to be different than she is, her anxiety healed, and she felt peaceful for the first time in her life. She is now exploring what her passion and purpose really is rather than trying to fit herself in what she believed she should be.

Learn to Dialogue with Your Inner Child

Now that you have begun to meet your wounded self and your true self, you can learn to dialogue with them for healing. When doing an Inner Bonding process, it's important not to skip any steps. Here we will be reviewing steps 1 and 2, because each time you do an Inner Bonding process, you need to take the time to do each step fully before moving on to the next step. The more you practice each step, the more natural it will become to do these steps in order and the more you will see why it's so important not to skip a step.

Start with step 1, breathing into your body, scanning your body for physical sensations, getting present with your feelings, and making a conscious decision that you want responsibility for your feelings.

Move into step 2, putting your hands on your heart, breathing into your heart, consciously choosing the intent to learn about loving yourself, and inviting the presence of your Divine guidance—of love and compassion—into your heart. Invite your Divine guidance to be with you as you explore, so that you can be a loving adult with your inner child and with your wounded self.

Now that you are present with your feelings and you are operating as a loving adult in this moment, you can move into the dialogue processes that are step 3. If you are feeling wounded feelings, such as anxiety, stress, depression, anger, guilt, shame, aloneness, emptiness, jealousy, rage, or resentment, ask your inner child the following questions.

What am I telling you that is causing these feelings?

How am I treating you that is causing these feelings?

What am I doing or not doing that is causing you to feel this way?

What am I doing that is making you feel rejected and abandoned by me and that is causing these feelings?

After asking these questions from your loving adult, breathe inside your body, breathing into the places of emotional or physical pain. Focus inside, allowing the answers to come from within—from the feelings—not from your mind.

Now, ask the questions, go inside, and write what your inner child wants to tell you.

_____

_____

_____

_____

If you are unclear, ask more questions. For example, if your inner child says, "You are judging me. You don't listen to me, and you put a lot of pressure on me," you can ask, "What am I saying when I'm judging you?" "What am I not hearing that you need me to hear?" "What is the pressure I'm putting on you about?" Keep going deeper, asking questions from your loving adult and allowing your inner child to answer.

ADULT:

_____

_____

_____

CHILD:

_____

_____

_____

ADULT:

_____

_____

_____

CHILD:

_____

_____

_____

If you need more room for the dialogue, please take out some paper and continue.

Learn to Dialogue with Your Wounded Self

Once you feel clear about what you are telling yourself, how you are treating yourself, what you are doing or not doing, and the various ways you are rejecting and abandoning yourself, you are ready to go to the next level of the dialogue process and explore your wounded self to discover the beliefs behind your unloving, self-abandoning behavior.

When you talk to your wounded self, be sure to be compassionate, because your wounded self has good reasons for what it's doing. You need to voice whatever your inner child told you that you are doing that's causing the wounded feelings (judging, criticizing, numbing with addictions, and so on). For example, if you have discovered that the reason your inner child feels depressed is because you are ignoring his or her feelings, you can ask your wounded self, "What are you trying to control or avoid by ignoring our feelings?"

Now go ahead and ask, "There must be some good reasons why you are treating the inner child this way. What are you, my wounded self, trying to control or avoid feeling by

_____ ?"

Allow the wounded self to answer. These answers will come from your mind—not from your body, because the false beliefs are housed in the lower part of the brain. For example, the wounded self might say, "I'm trying to avoid rejection by being perfect. If I'm perfect, I can control how others feel about me" or "I can't handle the pain of loneliness, so I have to eat junk to avoid it." Or "I can control others by getting angry and blaming them." Remember: stay curious and open to learning with no judgment!

_____

_____

_____

_____

_____

_____

Once you get a clear understanding of a false belief that is fueling your self-abandoning behavior, you might want to move on to dialoguing with your Divine guidance to discover the truth about the belief. You will learn to dialogue with Divine guidance in the next chapter, which covers step 4, but I mention it here because when you are actually dialoguing, you might go back and forth between steps 3 and 4, discovering a false belief and then going right to your guidance for the truth, and then back to step 3 for more exploration of beliefs. But before we move on to that, there is more work to do regarding false beliefs.

Exploring an Issue in Writing

Decide on a current issue that you want to explore. It might be a relationship issue or a parenting, work, or health issue. It might be about an addiction or about speaking your truth to someone. Tune in to whatever is currently challenging for you.

The issue I want to explore is:

_____

_____

_____

Become present in your body with your feelings about the issue and decide you want responsibility for those feelings. Then breathe into your heart, consciously choosing the intent to learn about what is loving to you, and invite the presence of your guidance into your heart.

Ask your inner child what you are telling yourself and how you are treating yourself around this issue that is causing any distress.

ADULT: What am I telling you and how am I treating you concerning this issue?

CHILD: _____

_____

_____

Keep asking questions until you get a clear understanding of your participation in the issue.

ADULT: _____

_____

CHILD: _____

_____

ADULT: _____

_____

CHILD: _____

_____

ADULT: _____

_____

CHILD: _____

_____

Once you are clear on what you are telling yourself or doing, dialogue with your wounded self to discover the fears and beliefs leading to any self-abandonment. It's often helpful to tune in to how old the wounded self is that is operating in this issue. Remember, your wounded self can be any age, depending on when you absorbed a false belief or learned a self-abandoning behavior.

This where you start to tune in to your fears and the false beliefs that are fueling your fears regarding a particular issue that is a problem for you.

ADULT: There must be a good reason you are saying these things to the inner child or treating the inner child in these unloving ways. Can you tell me why you are doing this?

WOUNDED SELF: I'm afraid of _____

_____

WOUNDED SELF: I believe that _____

_____

_____

_____

Then tune in to the past and recall experiences that led to the self-abandoning behavior.

ADULT: How did you get these beliefs? Where did you learn these behaviors?

WOUNDED SELF: _____

_____

_____

_____

_____

_____

You go on with this dialogue until you have a good understanding of the fears and beliefs behind your self-abandoning behavior.

Take a moment to visualize your Divine guidance and ask, "What is the truth about any of these beliefs I've uncovered?" and "What is the loving action toward my inner child?" Allow the answers to come through you. They don't need to be accurate—just write whatever pops into your mind.

_____

_____

_____

_____

_____

Be gentle with yourself. Talk encouragingly and supportively to yourself. Paying attention to your thinking and to how you are treating yourself can make all the difference in your life, as it did for Rosalee.

Rosalee grew up in a judgmental and critical family, and that was how she thought about herself and others for many years. Through her inner work, she realized what she was doing and why she felt so low. She started to pay attention to her thinking and consciously started to choose more loving ways to relate to herself. The more she noticed and the more she changed the way she talked to herself, the more her self-talk shifted from speaking and thinking in judgmental and critical ways to compassionate and uplifting ways, until it became a habit. Now she is aware of when her wounded self is judging, and she is able to shift her thinking.

"Years ago this idea of talking with myself and nurturing myself felt strange. I needed nurturing from others so badly, and because most of the time I didn't get it, I felt bad about myself. I depended on others for how I was feeling. Not anymore! Now I just love to be loving and compassionate to myself, and my inner child appreciates it and smiles most of the time."

Out-Loud Dialoguing

Take some time to go through the same kind of process as you did above—perhaps with a different issue that you want to explore—but this time do it out loud, either in your home or, preferably, while you are sitting or walking out in nature. It's important to discover how you like to dialogue and what works best for you. I live in a rural area, so when I do this while walking, no one—except my dogs—hears me when I'm talking out loud. If you live in a city and you want to dialogue out loud, just put ear buds in your ears and hold your cell phone and no one will know you are talking to yourself or think you are crazy! I also encourage you to dialogue out loud in the shower, since water sometimes makes it easier to connect. I also dialogue out loud if I'm alone in my car and stuck in traffic.

Ask About the Six Major Areas of Self-Abandonment

I have discovered that there are six major areas where we need to be taking personal responsibility for ourselves in order for our inner child to feel loved, peaceful, and safe: our *emotional*, *physical*, *financial*, *relational*, *organizational*, and *spiritual* lives. You may be taking responsibility for yourself as a loving adult in some areas but abandoning yourself in others. Self-abandonment in any of these areas may cause you to feel stressed and may make it harder to connect with your Divine guidance.

Emotional Self-Abandonment

You emotionally reject and abandon yourself whenever you ignore your feelings by staying focused in your head, turning to addictions to numb your feelings, judging yourself, or making others responsible for your feelings. What are you doing that makes your inner child feel stressed, rejected, and emotionally abandoned by you?

Ask your inner child, "In general, how do I treat you that makes you feel stressed, anxious, depressed, angry, guilty, ashamed, alone, and unloved within?" Breathe inside and let your inner child answer.

_____

_____

_____

_____

_____

Ask your wounded self, "What are your fears and beliefs that lead us to be resistant to taking emotional responsibility?"

_____

_____

_____

_____

Ask your inner child, "How do you generally feel when I'm emotionally abandoning you?"

_____

_____

_____

_____

Ask your inner child, "What do you want me to be doing differently so that you feel seen, heard, valued, and emotionally supported by me?"

_____

_____

_____

_____

_____

Physical Self-Abandonment

There are five major ways you might be abandoning yourself physically:

- *food*: avoiding responsibility for feeding yourself clean, high-vibrancy foods, and using food addictively—or starving yourself—to avoid your feelings

- *exercise*: sitting too much, not getting the exercise you need, or overexercising

- *sleep*: not making sure you are getting enough sleep

- *weight*: keeping yourself too thin or too heavy for health

- *safety*: for example, not wearing a helmet when riding a motorcycle or not wearing a seat belt in a car

Ask your inner child, "How do I treat you regarding food, exercise, sleep, and safety? Am I feeding you foods that make you feel bad? Am I using junk food to avoid your feelings and fill your emptiness? Am I starving you or making you vomit up our food? Am I making you be too thin, or judging you for being too fat? Do I listen to you regarding exercise? Are we getting enough sleep? What do I do to cause you stress regarding our health and physical safety?" Breathe inside and let your inner child answer.

_____

_____

_____

_____

If you are not taking loving care of yourself physically, ask your wounded self, "What are your fears and beliefs that lead us to be resistant to taking physical responsibility?"

_____

_____

_____

If you are not taking physical responsibility, ask your inner child, "How do you feel when I don't take physical care of you?"

_____

_____

_____

Ask your inner child, "What do you want me to be doing differently so that you feel loved by me regarding your physical health, safety, and well-being?"

_____

_____

_____

Financial Self-Abandonment

Money issues can cause much stress. Financial self-abandonment generally falls into seven areas:

- *spending addictively*: spending too much on things you don't need and putting yourself into debt

- *rigid spending limits*: not allowing yourself to enjoy your money when money is abundant or trying to control others regarding money

- *working*: working too much or too little

- *obsessing*: worrying about finances even when you have plenty of money

- *giving yourself up*: caretaking others financially when they need to be taking care of themselves

- *dependency*: allowing yourself to be financially dependent when you could be earning money (unless you are disabled or ill, or staying home with young children)

- *ignoring*: keeping yourself in the dark by avoiding knowing about your financial situation

Ask your inner child, "How am I taking care of you—or not taking care of you—financially? Am I spending too much or too little? Am I working too hard or not hard enough? Am I making you feel safe or stressed? Am I giving myself up or being financially dependent? Am I in the dark about our finances? What do I do to cause you stress regarding money?" Breathe inside and let your inner child answer.

_____

_____

_____

_____

If you are not taking loving care of yourself financially, ask your wounded self, "What are your fears and beliefs that lead us to be resistant to taking financial responsibility?"

_____

_____

_____

_____

If you are not taking financial responsibility for yourself, ask your inner child, "How do you feel when I don't take financial responsibility?"

_____

_____

_____

Ask your inner child, "What do you want me to be doing differently so that you feel safe financially?"

_____

_____

_____

_____

Relationship Self-Abandonment

Our relationships offer us an amazing opportunity for learning and growth, because they trigger everything that is unhealed in us. Because of this and because our relationships are so important in our lives, this section is much longer than the other five sections on self-abandonment.

When it comes to romantic relationships, people want to be in a relationship for one of two reasons: either they want to get love, approval, validation, and a sense of worth or they want to learn and grow together and share love with each other. The wounded self wants to get love, while the loving adult and your inner child want to share love.

If you are looking to be in a relationship, why do you want to be in a relationship? What are you hoping for in a relationship?

_____

_____

_____

_____

If you are in a relationship, what is your primary intent for being in the relationship?

_____

_____

_____

_____

One of our biggest challenges is to show up for ourselves in relationship with those people who are important to us—parents, children, our partner, close relatives, close friends, employees, employers, and professionals such as your doctor, attorney, or therapist. When the fear of losing the other person or of them being angry, disapproving, or rejecting is greater than the fear of losing yourself, you will tend to try to control them rather than focus on loving yourself. When you do this, the message to your inner child is that he or she isn't important enough for you to love yourself—and that getting love or approval is more important than being loving to yourself and to others.

Ask your inner child, "How am I taking care of you—or not taking care of you—in our important relationships? Do I speak up for you, or do I compromise you? Do I try to control others with anger, blame, defensiveness, compliance, resistance, withdrawal, or other forms of control rather than lovingly attending to you? Am I making others responsible for your worth, safety, and happiness? What do I do to cause you stress regarding our interactions with others?" Breathe inside, and let your inner child answer.

_____

_____

_____

_____

_____

If you are not taking loving care of yourself in your important relationships, ask your wounded self, "What are your fears and beliefs that lead us to be resistant to taking relationship responsibility?"

_____

_____

_____

_____

_____

If you are not taking relationship responsibility, ask your inner child, "How do you feel when I don't take relationship responsibility? How do you feel when I abandon you by making someone else responsible for your happiness, safety, and worth?"

_____

_____

_____

_____

Ask your inner child, "What do you want me to be doing differently regarding taking loving care of you within our relationships?"

_____

_____

_____

_____

Ellen, in her early forties, consulted with me because her boyfriend, Fred, had left her, and she was devastated. While she wasn't aware of it, Ellen had completely abandoned herself to Fred, making him responsible for her happiness and her sense of safety and worth—as she had done in all her relationships. In her mind, her relationship with Fred was the best relationship she had ever had, and she was deeply hurt and confused that he ended it.

Fortunately, Ellen was tired of getting hurt in her relationships, and she became open to learning about her various forms of self-abandonment. She learned that because she was abandoning herself, she had been trying to control Fred with her anger and neediness, hoping he would see how much she needed him to show her that he loved her in order for her to feel that she was lovable.

As a result of Ellen's learning to love and value herself, Ellen and Fred are starting to spend time together again. Ellen is now able to care about Fred, rather than always trying to have control over getting him to care about her.

All relationships have a system, especially relationships with a partner or spouse. Sometimes the system is healthy, but too often it's dysfunctional. A common relationship system that often causes problems is the *caretaker-taker system.* You can be a caretaker in some areas, and a taker in others. For example, you can be a caretaker financially and a taker sexually.

Are you sometimes a caretaker, giving yourself up to take responsibility for your partner's inner child, and then eventually feeling resentful and drained that your partner isn't doing for you what you do for him or her? And are you sometimes a taker, making your partner responsible for your feelings and getting angry when he or she doesn't do it right?

In what areas are you a caretaker?

_____

_____

_____

_____

In what areas are you a taker?

_____

_____

_____

_____

When you are operating as a taker or a caretaker, you are operating from your wounded self. Both these aspects of a codependent system come from self-abandonment.

How do you feel when you are operating as a taker or a caretaker?

_____

_____

_____

_____

What happens in your relationship when you are operating as a caretaker or a taker?

_____

_____

_____

_____

People are attracted to each other at their common level of woundedness, which is their common level of self-abandonment. People who are mostly loving themselves aren't going to be attracted to someone who is mostly self-abandoning. Often, it's much easier to see your partner's wounded self than to see your own and to blame your partner for your unhappiness, but if you accept that you are both operating from a common level of self-abandonment, it's easier to take your eyes off your partner, focus on yourself, and explore your participation in your relationship system.

There are numerous other kinds of relationship systems that are based on control rather than on love. Perhaps you have a relationship system in which you both try to control with anger and blame. There tends to be a lot of fighting in this system, with each partner being reactive and blaming the other person for the problems. This may create a lot of juice due to the intensity of the arguing, but eventually this is quite wearing on both partners and both end up feeling unloved.

Perhaps one of you is angry much of the time and the other is withdrawn or resistant, withholding your love as a covert form of punishment or shutting down to protect against being controlled by your partner. Each partner blames the other: "If only she wasn't so angry,

I wouldn't avoid her so much" and "If only he didn't always shut me out and wasn't so stubborn, I wouldn't be so angry." Both are right, and both are wrong. They are right in that each of them can change the system by learning to love themselves and share their love. They are wrong in that they each came into the relationship with their learned ways of controlling already developed, and the other person doesn't cause them to react the way they do.

Perhaps both of you are caretakers, trying to gain each other's approval by giving yourselves up. This is generally a calm system and may look like a loving system, but when the giving has an agenda, it's a covert form of control. This system generally lacks the juice necessary for true intimacy.

Sometimes both people have cut their loses and are withdrawn, which is a flat, disconnected, and generally boring system. They don't want to leave and be alone, but the system is too unsafe to be open and honest with each other.

A loving system evolves in a relationship when each person takes responsibility for loving themselves and filling themselves with love to share with the other. In a loving system, each partner is focused on kindness toward themselves and the other. They want their own highest good and the highest good of their partner. In conflict, they are both open to learning about themselves and the other, utilizing conflict as a learning opportunity. Neither tries to dominate the other into caving in and giving themselves up. Both stay open to learning with whatever comes up between them. They feel safe in sharing their feelings and needs with each other.

In a loving system, because learning and growth are important to each person, the relationship stays alive. Their attraction for each other grows through the new learning that is always occurring within themselves and with each other. They have fun together, they are secure in knowing that the other person has their back, and intimacy flourishes.

If you are currently in a relationship, what is your relationship system and how do you feel about this system? If you are currently not in a relationship, describe your past relationship systems and how you felt about them.

_____

_____

_____

_____

If you have any system other than a loving system, are you ready to risk learning to love yourself and shift your system? If not, what are you afraid of? What do you believe will happen if you learn to love yourself?

_____

_____

_____

_____

People often ask me when to leave a relationship. What I say is that unless there is physical or emotional abuse, it's best to hang in and work on your own end of the relationship system until you feel happy and peaceful within. You don't want to take your dysfunctional patterns into another relationship. Once you feel happy and peaceful within, if the relationship isn't healing, it may be time to leave, if that is what you want. However, often when one person heals their end of the relationship system, the whole system heals.

What do you see as your part of the system that you need to heal?

_____

_____

_____

_____

_____

A common conflict issue in relationships is sexuality, especially over the frequency of sex.

Being honest with yourself, ask yourself, when you want to have sex, why do you want to? Do you want to have sex to get something such as validation or stress release or to give and share love and connection?

_____

_____

_____

_____

Sometimes wanting sex is a control issue.

Jennifer consulted with me because she was confused about the sexual problems in her marriage. For years, her husband, Adam, would get angry if she didn't want to have sex with him, and he had frequently complained that she never initiated sex. Most of the time, Jennifer gave in to his demands to avoid his anger. But she rarely initiated sex.

When Jennifer reached her mid-thirties, her sex drive increased, and she started to initiate sex with Adam. To her great surprise, he withdrew, suddenly not interested in having sex. "I don't get this," she said to me. "I'm giving him what he said he wanted, and now he isn't interested."

I said, "That's because, even though Adam thought he wanted you to initiate sex, what he really wants is control. He loses control when you initiate sex. Try pulling back again and see what happens."

The next week a very surprised Jennifer showed up for her Skype session. "I don't believe this. As soon as I pulled back, he started to pull on me for sex and again complained about me not initiating. I feel like I can't win."

"You can't," I said. "This isn't actually a sexual issue. Like I said last week, it's a control issue. Getting angry at you for not having sex is about control. Pulling back when you initiate sex is about control. Are there other areas in your marriage in which he gets angry or withdraws?"

"Yes!" she said. "He does the same thing with money. He spends what he wants but gets angry and pouty when I buy something without getting his approval, even though I make more money than he does!"

Fortunately, Adam was willing to have couples counseling with Jennifer and address their system, in which he tried to control her with anger and withdrawal, and Jennifer tried to control his anger with her compliance. Their relationship gradually improved as they each learned to take responsibility for their feelings, rather than make the other responsible.

Wanting sex to share love comes from a completely different place inside than sex to get something. In order to have love and connection to share, you have to already be connected with yourself and feel filled with love. You cannot share something that you don't already have. And you cannot share love and connection when you feel unhappy, empty, inadequate, unlovable, disconnected from yourself, stressed, agitated, angry, or wanting to feel in control of your partner.

If you and your partner are having sexual problems, you each may want to examine the system between you. Is there a pull-resist system? Is there a pull-compliance system? Is there a compliance-compliance system? Any of these systems may be bypassing the true sharing of love and joy that sexuality between loving, caring partners offers.

Ask your inner child, "What do you want me to be doing differently regarding our sexual relationship or what did you want me to do differently in our past relationships?"

_____

_____

_____

_____

A common complaint among people who are seeking a relationship is that they keep attracting unavailable partners. If you find yourself in this situation over and over, you need to explore your *own* unavailability. Relationship unavailability generally comes from two major fears:

- fear of rejection—of losing the other

- fear of engulfment—of losing yourself

When you don't have a loving adult to help you lovingly manage rejection, you might be too afraid of getting hurt to be open to a relationship. While you know you want to be in a relationship, your wounded self might be putting up barriers out of the fear of getting hurt. If your primary fear is of engulfment, then as soon as you get close to someone, the fear of losing yourself might surface, and you find yourself uninterested in the other person. If you tend to give yourself up out of the fear of rejection, your inner child won't trust you to not lose yourself in the relationship, and you will find yourself backing away.

If you consistently attract unavailable people or you find yourself backing away from relationships as you start to feel close, what are you most afraid of?

_____

_____

_____

_____

Ask your inner child, "How do I reject and abandon you when we start to like someone that makes you scared of getting rejected and hurt or scared of losing yourself in a relationship?"

_____

_____

_____

_____

Ask your inner child, "What do you need from me regarding a partner rejecting me—or trying to control and engulf me—to no longer be afraid to be in a relationship?"

_____

_____

_____

_____

In order to sustain a healthy relationship, you need to learn to manage the loneliness, heartbreak, and helplessness of rejection. No matter how good a relationship, there is always going to be rejection. There is no such thing as a relationship in which you never feel the hurt of rejection. In order to learn to manage the pain of rejection so that you won't give yourself up, you need to develop your loving adult self, who can speak up for you and help you not take rejection personally, as well as bring in Spirit to comfort the heartache. You need to become strong enough to keep your heart open in the face of rejection and strong enough to be willing to lose the other person rather than lose yourself.

Organizational Self-Abandonment

Organizational self-abandonment is about not taking responsibility regarding time and space, such as always being late, not paying bills on time, and keeping home and work spaces cluttered or disorganized.

Ask your inner child, "How am I taking care of you, or not taking care of you, regarding time and space? Am I always late or am I on time regarding events, meetings, bills, and taxes? Do I keep our home, car, and workspaces peaceful and clean, or are they messy, disorganized, and cluttered? What do I do to cause you stress regarding time and space?" Breathe inside, and let your inner child answer.

_____

_____

_____

_____

_____

_____

If you are not taking loving care of yourself regarding time or space, ask your wounded self, "What are your fears and beliefs that lead us to be resistant to taking organizational responsibility?"

_____

_____

_____

_____

Ask your inner child, "How do you feel when we are late for appointments or in paying bills or taxes, or when our home, office, or car are messy and cluttered? How do you feel when I'm resistant to taking organizational responsibility?"

_____

_____

_____

_____

Ask your inner child, "What do you want me to be doing differently regarding time and space?"

_____

_____

_____

_____

Spiritual Self-Abandonment

You are abandoning yourself spiritually when you don't take the time to connect with your guidance through prayer, meditation, or your Inner Bonding practice and when you put your wounded self in charge of your decisions rather than your guidance. When you don't tune in to the love, comfort, and wisdom of your Divine guidance, you are allowing your inner child to be spiritually abandoned.

Ask your inner child, "How am I taking care of you, or not taking care of you, spiritually? Do I give you time to be with our guidance or not? Am I allowing our wounded self to make our choices—or our guidance? Am I tuning in to truth, or am I allowing the lies of our wounded self to scare you? Do I bring love and comfort from Spirit to you? What do I do to cause you stress regarding our Divine connection?" Breathe inside, and let your inner child answer.

_____

_____

_____

_____

If you are not taking loving care of yourself spiritually, ask your wounded self, "What are your fears and beliefs that lead us to be resistant to taking spiritual responsibility?"

_____

_____

_____

If you are not taking spiritual responsibility, ask your inner child, "How do you feel when I don't take spiritual responsibility?"

_____

_____

_____

As your inner child, "What do you want me to be doing differently regarding our spiritual connection?"

_____

_____

_____

Discover What Brings You Joy

You don't have to wait for a problem to dialogue with your inner child. In fact, a wonderful time to discover what your inner child loves to do and what brings you joy is when you are feeling happy and peaceful. At this point in my life, since I've been practicing Inner Bonding for so long, most of the time when I take my morning walk and check in with my feelings, I'm feeling wonderful. I then ask my inner child what she wants to do on the weekend, whom she wants to play with, what she would like to paint (I'm a painter and a potter), or what kind of pots she wants to make when we have time in my studio.

I also open to learning with my Divine guidance on my walks, asking an open-ended question: "What would you like to tell me?" Often I receive new ideas for articles or books to write or insights into things I've been thinking about.

At a time when you are feeling peaceful and connected with your feelings and your guidance, and after doing the first two steps of Inner Bonding, ask your inner child questions such as, "What would you like to do this weekend?" or "What's fun for you?" or "Whom would you like to spend time with?" or "How do you feel about _____?" or any questions regarding what your inner child likes and wants. Go inside and allow the answers to come from within, not from your mind.

_____

_____

_____

_____

You can also ask questions such as "What kind of books do you like to read?" (My child and my adult like different kinds of books, so I'm usually reading two books at a time!) and "What are your favorite colors?" and "What style clothing do you like?" Sometimes your adult self makes the choices, and at other times, you might want to let your inner child make the choices.

_____

_____

_____

_____

You can also ask about the kind of exercise your inner child likes. Part of keeping your frequency high is moving enough. Sitting a lot lowers your frequency. Sometimes your lifestyle, such as if you live on a farm, naturally provides enough movement, and this is ideal. But if you sit a lot, getting enough exercise is vital for keeping your frequency high. To be consistent in exercising, the exercise needs to be something you love and look forward to doing.

Ask your inner child, "What kind of movement or exercise do you love?"

_____

_____

_____

_____

Creative activities, such as arts, crafts, playing an instrument, writing, acting, inventing, building, and the like, can be fulfilling. Ask your inner child, "What kind of creative activities do you like?"

_____

_____

_____

_____

Beginning to Discover Your Blueprint for Your Passionate Purpose

"I can't seem to discover why I'm on the planet."

"What is my purpose here? I know there's something I'm supposed to be doing, but I don't know how to find out what it is."

"I don't seem to be passionate about anything."

I've heard these complaints over and over from my clients. We are born with a blueprint for what we came to the planet to share and express. This blueprint is part of our essence—our inner child. Some people know early in life what their passion and purpose is, while others need to discover this later, because the blueprint got buried during their childhood. If your true self was not seen and validated by your parents, teachers, or other caregivers, it may have gone underground, along with the blueprint for your passion and purpose. You can't discover your passion and purpose from your wounded self, because this part of you doesn't have access to what is true for your soul essence.

How, then, do you discover your passion and purpose, if the blueprint for this information is long buried? The good news is that while it might be buried, it's not lost. You can reclaim this information if you are willing to do your Inner Bonding work.

I've worked with thousands of clients who, as they practice Inner Bonding, gradually heal their fears and false beliefs to the point that their true self starts to emerge. This vital, alive, loving aspect of yourself wants to joyfully express itself in the world. As you allow this aspect to emerge, you will gradually discover not only what truly brings you joy but also what you came to this planet to lovingly offer.

Were you encouraged to ignore your special talents and instead choose your career according to what would give you a sense of security? Too often, what makes you feel safe does not fulfill you emotionally or spiritually.

> Glenn worked for many years as an attorney, but he never enjoyed it. He made a lot of money, yet when he consulted with me, he was suffering from anxiety and depression. He had become an attorney because his father had been an attorney and had wanted Glenn to follow in his footsteps. Glenn had gone along with what his father wanted for him because he didn't know what else he wanted, and now, in midlife, he was miserable. He yearned to discover his passion.

As Glenn was dialoguing with his inner child, he remembered that he had really wanted to be a college professor. He had never seriously considered this career, because he felt he couldn't make enough money at it, but now he was willing to make far less money, because he was so unhappy with his present work. Glenn went back to school and eventually got a job teaching English at a university. The last time I spoke with him he was radiant! He loved working with young people, and he felt he was making a real contribution to their lives. For the first time ever, he felt alive and passionate about his life. Furthermore, his wife had decided to take up some of the financial slack by doing something she had always wanted to do: designing children's clothing. She started her own mail-order business and was thrilled with it. Their marriage and family life are flourishing because both of them are happy and fulfilled within themselves.

While it may not always be possible to change your work immediately to something you love, if you follow your passion, it can lead you there. And even if you have to earn money in ways that do not express your soul, you can seek volunteer opportunities and hobbies to express who you are. Often these can lead to the work that you will eventually do.

Luis worked as a manager of a large supermarket. With his small savings, he decided to start pursuing a hobby that had always fascinated him—restoring old cars. He used all his extra money to buy his first old car and spent many blissful hours restoring it. He was so good at it that he was able to sell his restored cars for a big profit. Eventually, he was able to quit his job at the market and pursue his passion full time. Ultimately he started a project in a prison, teaching inmates to restore cars. Luis now loves what he does and receives great satisfaction from helping others.

Your soul has a deep desire for you to express yourself in ways that are deeply fulfilling to you. You can discover what that is and bring it to life through inner dialoguing.

At a time when you know you are in your loving adult state and you are feeling peaceful and connected with your inner child and your guidance, ask your inner child, "If we could snap our fingers and instantly be doing work you would love, what would you love to do?" Go inside and allow the answer to come from within, and answer in writing or out loud. Don't worry about it being the right answer. Just write or say whatever emerges from within. If nothing comes, let that be okay. Eventually, if you keep learning to be a loving adult, your inner child will let you in on the blueprint.

_____

_____

_____

_____

Open to learning with your Divine guidance and ask, "What do you want to tell me about my passion and purpose?" Then let go, and write or speak out loud whatever pops into your mind. Again, if nothing comes, let that be okay. I assure you that at some point, you will start to receive answers about this.

_____

_____

_____

_____

Spend some time talking with people who are doing what you think you would love to do, and do research in areas of life that interest you. Who are the people you have always admired regarding what they do in the world?

_____

_____

_____

What kind of books do you tend to gravitate to in a bookstore?

_____

_____

_____

The answers to these questions can give you hints regarding what your blueprint is for your passionate purpose.

Brandon felt lost. He appeared to be a big, gruff, tough guy, with a lot of armor over his heart. "I have a family to support, but it's so hard to get myself to work. Maybe I'm just a lazy person. Our parents are helping us financially, but I can't rely on them forever, and I know I need to be earning money. But most of the time I feel too depressed to work. There must be something wrong with me."

Brandon was working part-time at an accounting firm, helping with bookkeeping. He hated it. When I asked him if there is anything he really enjoys doing, he immediately said, "I love growing organic fruits and vegetables. I have a big garden that I love, and it's been really helping to feed our family. I've even had produce to sell to a few people, and I love knowing that I'm contributing to their health. I love the idea of working and living together in a community with people supporting each other in being healthy."

In front of my eyes, Brandon transformed from a depressed, armored, gruff guy to an alive and vibrant man.

"Brandon, this is your passion! Why aren't you doing this as your work?"

"I didn't think it was okay to do this as my work. I thought I was supposed to be doing other work. And I'm not sure how to get the land I need to do this work."

As we explored, Brandon came up with some ideas regarding how to get the land he needs. He also went online and found a job advertised for work on an organic farm. He called immediately and got hired! He also looked into taking online classes on organic, sustainable farming and registered for one. This was one excited man! Brandon wasn't lazy—he was bored and depressed over not expressing his passion and purpose. His inner child was obviously delighted with his new decisions!

Everyone has a blueprint for his or her passionate purpose, so be assured that you will discover yours as you practice Inner Bonding and develop your loving adult.

Step 4

Dialogue with Your Divine Guidance

Our Divine guidance is always here for us when our frequency is high enough to access it. As you let go of junk foods and junk thoughts and replace them with healthy foods and thoughts based on love and truth, your frequency becomes high enough to have two-way, at-will communication with your personal source of spiritual guidance. Your Divine guidance becomes your source of wisdom, love, and comfort and is your primary role model for loving action.

In this step, you will ask your Divine guidance about the *truth regarding the false beliefs* you uncovered in step 3, and what *loving actions* you can take for your inner child to feel happy and peaceful, with a sense of inner safety and self-worth. Even if your inner child has told you what he or she wants, you still need to open to learning with your Divine guidance regarding what actions would be loving to you, because your inner child may want something that your guidance says isn't in your highest good. It's not just about what you want; it's also about what is most loving to you. You can know what is truly loving to you when your feelings about what you want and what feels right to you are in agreement with the advice from your Divine guidance. This sense of alignment between your feelings and the information coming in from your Divine guidance is how you can know what is truly loving to you and in your highest good.

Discovering the Truth

You will know that you've accessed the truth by your feelings. Whenever I hear what I believe is the truth, I then check in with my feelings. The truth feels right and expansive within, while the false beliefs and lies of the wounded self create stress within. As I've previously stated, your feelings are unerring regarding knowing what's true and right for you, as well as what is not supportive of your highest good. Your positive feelings let you know you are on the right track.

When I first started practicing Inner Bonding, it often took days, weeks, or even months to access answers from my Divine guidance. Now, most of the time it happens instantly. When a deep issue comes up, it might take a few hours or even a day or two, but rarely longer than that. However, it took me a lot of practice to have this level of at-will access! Here is an exercise to get you started.

Go back to one of the dialogues you did in the last chapter—perhaps the dialogue you did in the section called "Exploring an Issue in Writing."

Write down the issue you are examining and the false beliefs from your wounded self that you uncovered.

The issue is: _____

The false beliefs I uncovered are: _____

_____

_____

_____

_____

With an intent to learn, ask your Divine guidance, "What is the truth about these false beliefs I uncovered?" Relax, let go, and write whatever pops into your mind about each belief. Don't censor or worry about whether what you are hearing or seeing is right—or whether you are making it up. It takes practice to clearly access your guidance, so start with just writing down whatever words, images, or ideas pop into your mind.

_____

_____

_____

_____

_____

If nothing comes, don't worry about it. Keep asking, especially when you are out in nature or just before falling asleep. Keep on the lookout for the answers, as they might come in a book you are reading, when you are in the shower, while speaking with a friend, in a dream, or in numerous other ways. Farina's story shows how transformative an ongoing dialogue with Divine guidance can be.

Farina comes from an extremely traumatic childhood, including physical, emotional, and sexual abuse. When I started to work with her, she was dissociated, which means that she was completely disconnected from her body and her feelings. She believed that she was a completely worthless person, which made her vulnerable to being controlled by others in her life. Her many forms of self-abandonment included caretaking others, blaming and shaming herself, and dissociating, which she had to learn as a child to survive. As a result, she suffered from extreme anxiety.

She worked hard internally on creating her Divine connection, which has now become the most important aspect of her daily life. She now knows she is loved and held by Spirit, and she draws on it for ongoing support. Since learning how to tune in to her guidance, her anxiety almost completely disappeared. When anxiety resurfaces, it is usually related to old fears from the deep wounding that occurred in her childhood, which is sometimes triggered during the course of an ordinary day. When this happens, she asks her Divine guidance for help to perceive the truth about what she is feeling. It is often connected to an old belief that she hasn't yet worked through. Her dialoguing helps her see that the belief comes from old perceptions that are no longer valid for who she today.

"Before, I would pass through an entire day with anything from low-grade anxiety to full-blown anxiety and panic attacks. I didn't have a system or the tools that were deep enough to pull me out of the wounded states of fear that I had lived with for so long and that were ruling my life. With access to Divine guidance, I can consistently learn new ways of being."

As I stated in the last chapter, when you are dialoguing, you may want to go back and forth between step 3 and step 4. Sometimes you might want to ask your Divine guidance about the truth of a belief right away and then go back to doing some more exploration. It's important for Inner Bonding to be a fluid process, not a rigid "I hope I'm doing this right" kind of process.

Accessing Loving Action

I rarely saw my parents take loving action for themselves. Instead, they blamed each other for their feelings and gave themselves up to each other with the hope that the other would take care of them, and they were then angry and resentful when this didn't happen. I certainly could not use my parents as role models. It was also disconcerting to realize that, with all the therapy I had, no one ever helped me learn how to discover the loving action in any given situation. Looking back, I understand the reason they didn't help me: they didn't know how.

There is no simple formula for loving action. Clients often ask me, "What should I do in this situation?" I'd love to be able to answer them, but each situation is different. To know what to do in any particular situation, we need to be tuned in to our Divine guidance in the moment. As I got deeper into attempting to discover loving actions, I realized that Divine guidance needs to be the role model for each of us. Here are some questions you can pose to your Divine guidance to know what loving actions to take.

Ask your guidance questions like:

- "What is the loving behavior toward my inner child in this situation?"

- "What is in my highest good?"

- "What would be kind and caring to myself right now?"

Open and allow the answers to come through you in words, pictures, or feelings. Again, the answers may not come immediately, but if you have a sincere desire to learn, they will eventually come.

_____

_____

_____

_____

_____

_____

By staying open to learning, you will eventually have the experience of never being alone. This is where fears start falling away, and you begin to receive the love and wisdom you need to take loving action for yourself and with others. The process happens differently for each of us, as Victoria's story shows.

As they were for so many of us, Victoria's growing-up years were challenging. As a child, due to her upbringing, she had no sense of spiritual connection, so it took some years to develop. She knew that she wanted to connect, but she was afraid of opening up. Because she didn't trust her feelings or trust her loving adult to take loving action for her, she had no way to trust Divine guidance. She had grown up in an emotionally abusive environment and had learned to shut out whatever was going on around her and turn off her feelings so she could survive. But later she forgot that she was the one who had closed herself off, and she didn't realize that she was still protecting herself from what she most wanted, which was having a deeply meaningful relationship with her Divine guidance.

Victoria had much work to do on her relationship with Spirit, because she had many false beliefs that led to self-blame and guilt. She couldn't even imagine there being a source of love, wisdom, and guidance for her. Before she could trust that her higher power was here for her, she needed to do the work of creating her loving adult self, who could learn to connect with her Divine guidance and who could allow her inner child to relax and let the healing come through.

"Now, when I connect with my guidance at the beginning of my day, I hear something like, 'We love you immeasurably; we love you more than you could even possibly perceive. You can trust now; you are safe.' The love I feel now allows me to connect with the power of my own soul and to tune in to what is in my highest good."

Accessing Your Divine Guidance Through Dreamwork

Some people receive most of their guidance through their dreams. They find that if they ask a question before they go to sleep, the answer will often come through dreams. If you generally remember your dreams, you might discover them to be a source of profound information.

There are many different ways of working with dreams. You can write down your dreams when you wake up and then work with the dream by regarding each part of the dream as representing an aspect of yourself—your inner child, different aspects of your wounded self, your loving adult, and your Divine guidance. Try it for a night to see what happens.

Before you go to sleep, ask a question of your guidance.

The question I want to ask is: _____

_____

Have pen and paper handy, and as soon as you wake up, write down your dream.

_____

_____

_____

_____

_____

_____

_____

Go inside and tune in to what aspect of you each part of the dream represents.

- Inner child: _____

- Wounded self: _____

- Loving adult: _____

- Divine guidance: _____

Then have a dialogue with each part, asking what the part wants to tell you. You can receive much guidance by working with your dreams this way.

- My inner child is saying: _____

_____

- My wounded self is saying: _____

_____

- My loving adult is saying: _____

  _____

- My Divine guidance is saying: _____

  _____

Loving Actions in the Six Major Areas of Self-Responsibility

As you learned in the last chapter, we all need to learn to be a loving adult in six major areas of life. You might find yourself doing great in one area, such as taking physical responsibility, but you might be sorely lacking in taking emotional or financial responsibility. For your inner child to feel safe and loved, he or she needs you to learn to be a loving adult in all these areas. In step 3, you tuned in to how you might be abandoning yourself in these areas and explored some of the actions your inner child wants from you. Now it's time to ask your Divine guidance about loving actions in all these areas.

The areas of physical, financial, relationship, organizational, and spiritual responsibility all relate to the first area, emotional responsibility, because not taking responsibility in any of these areas causes pain, stress, and illness, and taking responsibility for them creates inner peace and the sense of safety sought in emotional responsibility.

Emotional Responsibility

In the previous step, we did some work on what your inner child wants from you emotionally. What does your guidance want to tell you regarding what loving actions you need to take so that your inner child feels seen, valued, loved, and safe? This is a lifelong process of becoming more and more aware of what it means to love yourself and then having the courage to take loving action.

Ask your guidance, "What loving action do I need to take right now for my inner child to feel emotionally loved by me?"

Let go and allow the words, feelings, or images to flow into you. Stay as open and present as you can. This is a layered process that you can keep doing over and over in your life.

_____

_____

_____

_____

Remember that whatever you have been wanting emotionally from others to feel loved, worthy, valued, and safe is what your inner child may be needing from you.

Ask your guidance, "What do I need to do in this moment to release stress and feel peaceful?"

_____

_____

_____

_____

Whenever you feel anything less than peaceful within, you might want to notice if there are background self-judgments or complaints coming from your wounded self. Once you notice these forms of negative thinking, try immediately expressing gratitude for something in the moment, and then smile about it. Gratitude opens the heart, and research shows that smiling activates endorphins. Then notice how you feel. You might be surprised!

Physical Responsibility

Divine connection occurs when our frequency is high, and how we treat ourselves physically has as much an impact on our frequency as how we treat ourselves emotionally.

Ask your Divine guidance, "What loving actions do I need to take regarding the food I eat to keep my frequency high?"

_____

_____

_____

_____

_____

Ask your Divine guidance, "What loving actions do I need to take regarding the purity of the water I drink and the nutrition of the fluids that I put into my body to keep my frequency high?"

_____

_____

_____

_____

Ask your Divine guidance, "What loving actions do I need to take regarding movement or exercise to keep my frequency high?"

_____

_____

_____

_____

Ask your Divine guidance, "What actions do I need to take regarding getting enough sleep to keep my frequency high?"

_____

_____

_____

_____

Ask your Divine guidance, "What actions do I need to take regarding physical safety to keep my frequency high?"

_____

_____

_____

_____

If you are suffering from one or more chronic conditions, you might want to consider seeing a functional medicine doctor. As I stated previously, conventional medicine is great for trauma such as broken bones or conditions that need surgery, but they have done little for chronic diseases and brain disorders, such as Alzheimer's, Parkinson's, heart disease, cancer, autoimmune diseases, fatigue, allergies, dementia, autism, and ADHD, as well as the anxiety and depression that comes from a toxic gut.

Functional medicine, which has been growing rapidly in the last ten years—thanks to Mark Hyman, MD, the founder of the Cleveland Clinic's Center for Functional Medicine, and to many other functional medicine practitioners, such as Chris Kresser, founder of the Kresser Institute and codirector of the California Center for Functional Medicine, who treat the root causes of chronic illness. Conventional medicine focuses on symptoms, not the causes, so chronic conditions are generally treated with drugs. Functional medicine doctors use different tests that detect the underlying causes of chronic conditions, and they have the knowledge of diet and lifestyle changes that are needed to slow down, reverse, or heal chronic disease.

While initially seeing a functional medicine practitioner may be more expensive than conventional medicine, because it's generally not covered by insurance (which gives the practitioners the freedom to order the necessary tests, rather than being controlled by the insurance companies), in the long run, it's far less costly.

If you are suffering from a chronic illness, are you motivated to make the diet and lifestyle changes you need to make? Yes: _____   No: _____

If your answer is no, why not? What fears and beliefs are in the way of taking this responsibility for your health?

_____

_____

_____

_____

If the answer is yes, but you don't currently have the funds to see a functional medicine doctor, are you willing to read the books that will teach you how to make some of the diet and lifestyle changes you need to make? Yes: _____   No: _____

If the answer is no, then you need to be honest with yourself that you don't want responsibility for your health. You might want to explore whether being ill is giving you some secondary gain, such as not having to take responsibility in other areas.

The secondary gain I experience from being ill is:

_____

_____

_____

_____

Ask your Divine guidance, "What is in my highest good regarding taking responsibility for my physical health?"

_____

_____

_____

Financial Responsibility

In the last chapter, you asked your inner child some questions about financial responsibility and about what your inner child wanted you to do. Now you need to ask your Divine guidance about what loving actions you need to take.

Ask your Divine guidance, "What loving actions do I need to take regarding finances to relieve stress and keep my frequency high?"

_____

_____

_____

_____

_____

_____

Relationship Responsibility

In relating with others, when we accept that we are helpless over their behavior, we are then free to take responsibility for our experience of being with them. Whom we are drawn to and whom we relate with, as well as how we relate with them, depend on how we relate with ourselves. The truth can be revealed through dialoguing, as Lily discovered.

Lily consistently chose unavailable men. When she was a child, her brother had been mean to her, and she became compliant as her way to attempt to control him. She was terrified of ending up with a man like her brother. She wanted to be in a relationship, so she asked her wounded self why she was attracted only to unavailable men, and she had the following dialogue.

WOUNDED SELF: A long time ago, I promised to protect you. My promise was that I would never, ever allow you to be treated like our brother treated us. I decided that it was safer for us to be alone—then no one can hurt us.

ADULT: Do you not believe that we could just say no to the men whom we don't feel safe around?

WOUNDED SELF: You rarely say no to anything. There is no way I can trust you to say no to an available man, so I allow you to attract and be attracted to men, but only men who are not willing or able to reciprocate toward you—unavailable men. I've been protecting you all these years, just as promised.

Lily reported to me that she had no idea she had these subconscious beliefs, because consciously she knows that there are many wonderful men out there. She then asked her Divine guidance another question.

ADULT: What loving actions can I take to become ready for an available man?

GUIDANCE: You need to practice speaking up for yourself in everyday situations, saying no instead of going along with what others want when it's not what you want. You will be attracted to available men when your inner child trusts you to speak up rather than be compliant.

For Lily, taking relationship responsibility meant healing her caretaking addiction and becoming a reliable advocate for her inner child, so that she was no longer attracting unavailable men due to her fears of rejection and engulfment.

Loving Actions in Relationship Conflict

All relationships have conflict. It's not the conflict that can cause problems—it's how you deal with conflict. There are only two loving actions you can take in conflict: *opening to learning* and *lovingly disengaging*. Here's the first, which is the best choice if you are able to open to learning, and you think the other person will also be open.

> You can state your feelings and open to learning with the other person, saying something like, "I'm feeling upset about what you are saying or doing, but I know you must have a good reason for saying it or for acting the way you are. Can we talk about this? I'd like to understand what's happening for you and if there is something I'm doing that is a part of the problem between us."

Being open to learning with another doesn't mean that you just want to understand them. It also means that you are open to learning about your participation in the system between you. As I stated in the last chapter, every relationship has a system, and learning about your role in that the system is a vital aspect of being open to learning in a relationship.

If you know that the other person will be closed to engaging with you, or if you are too upset to open to learning, here's the second loving action you can take.

> You need to lovingly disengage, which means you walk away with your heart open and focus on taking loving care of yourself and doing your own learning. This isn't the same as withdrawing, which is what we do when we close our heart in anger and withdraw our love to punish the other person. Withdrawal is a form of control, while lovingly disengaging is a way to get out of the line of fire or stop escalating the conflict, so you can take care of your feelings.

After you've lovingly disengaged and you've done your own Inner Bonding work, and you know that you are in an open state, check in with the other person to see if they are open to talking about the issue. If they are not open, you need to accept your helplessness over their intent and decide for yourself how to take loving care of yourself in the face of their unavailability. For example, once you embrace the loneliness and heartache caused by the other person being closed, what can you do that would be fun? Can you call or get together with a friend, do something creative, read a good book, get some exercise, meditate, do yoga, or dance? Do something that would feel loving to you, so you won't feel like a victim of the other person's closed heart.

Ask your guidance, "When someone important to me is angry, blaming, resistant, or withdrawn, what are the loving actions I need to take for myself?"

_____

_____

_____

_____

Ask your guidance, "When I'm feeling angry, blaming, resistant, defensive, righteous, withdrawn, or compliant, what loving action do I need to take for myself rather than act out from my wounded self? What loving action will keep my heart open and my frequency high?"

_____

_____

_____

_____

_____

A common area of conflict, especially in committed relationships, is sexuality. Feeling attracted to a partner and having your approaches reciprocated is frequently dependent on your relationship with yourself. Often our sexual struggles with another can be resolved when we take loving action toward ourselves, as Stanley discovered.

Stanley started to work with me because he was angry over the lack of a sex life with his wife, Angela. While Stanley and Angela loved each other and didn't want to end their marriage, Stanley was deeply frustrated that Angela had no interest in having sex with him. He believed that there was something wrong with Angela's sexuality. He was certain that their lack of sex was all her fault.

It soon become apparent that Stanley was using sex addictively—that is, he wanted sex with Angela when he was feeling empty inside or bad about himself. He wanted Angela to fill his emptiness and validate his worth. Stanley was addicted not only to sex but also to *self-judgment, which was causing his emptiness, neediness, and lack of self-worth. Whenever he judged himself, he would approach Angela from his wounded self, needy of sex to take away the emptiness, aloneness, and feelings of inadequacy that resulted from his self-judgments.*

There is nothing attractive or erotic about a partner coming for sex from a needy, wounded place. Angela knew from experience that she felt used and unfulfilled when she agreed to have sex with Stanley when he was needy. Angela was attracted to Stanley when he was coming from love, not from neediness.

As Stanley learned to love himself, rather than abandon himself with his self-judgments, he found that he no longer wanted to use Angela sexually to fill and validate himself. To his great surprise, Angela gradually became interested in reviving their sex life.

In step 3, you explored ways you might take responsibility for your sexuality in your relationship. If sexuality is an issue in your relationship, ask your Divine guidance for advice about loving actions.

Ask your guidance, "What is the loving action regarding our sexual conflict?"

_____

_____

_____

_____

You can ask this question regarding any conflict in a relationship. Each conflict provides much opportunity for learning about yourself and your partner, and when you turn to Divine guidance for new ways of learning and acting in the midst of conflict, you become more open to what is loving to both of you.

Organizational Responsibility

Organizing your time and space are important for a sense of inner peace and safety. If you are generally late to meetings or events, in paying bills and taxes, or in your work, or if your car or home is cluttered, this can create stress, which lowers your frequency.

Ask your guidance, "What loving actions do I need to take regarding my time to relieve stress and keep my frequency high?"

_____

_____

_____

_____

_____

Ask your guidance, "What loving actions do I need to take regarding my spaces to relieve stress and keep my frequency high?"

_____

_____

_____

_____

_____

Spiritual Responsibility

Taking spiritual responsibility means taking the time you need to learn to stay connected with your Divine guidance and building rituals—such as prayer, meditation, yoga, and practicing Inner Bonding—for spiritual connection. For example, my daily ritual is to start my day walking in nature, saying my prayers for loved ones and for the planet, expressing my gratitude for my many blessings, doing Inner Bonding dialogue work out loud, and then opening to learning about what my Divine guidance wants to tell me that day. This sets the tone for remembering to stay connected with my feelings and Divine guidance the rest of the day, as well as remembering to express gratitude throughout the day for big and small blessings.

Ask your guidance, "What is the most loving way for me to take spiritual responsibility so that I can keep my frequency high? What rituals would be loving to me to build into my life? What ceremonies would be helpful to me?"

_____

_____

_____

_____

Completing this section might result in a lot of to-dos that could feel overwhelming. As you prioritize and integrate them, give yourself permission to take them slowly. There is no rush to take these loving actions, so don't let your wounded self push you. You might want to pick the one that feels most important at this time. Focus on just that one until it has been integrated into your life. Then go through the list of actions again and pick another that feels important. Progress might be slower with some than with others, and it's important to make this okay. Pressuring yourself will likely result in resistance, which will stop you from developing the new habit of the loving action.

It takes time and practice to develop the new neurons in your higher brain for these loving actions. The more you remember to practice, the more progress you will make—but again, no judgment when you forget.

Bringing Spiritual Love and Comfort Inside

One of the most important loving actions we all need to learn to do is to fill ourselves up with the spiritual love and comfort that is always available to us. If we can't do this for ourselves, we will always be dependent on others, which means that we have no emotional freedom, and we can't act for our own benefit. And handing your inner child away for love and comfort will always make him or her feel abandoned. This doesn't mean that there is anything wrong with reaching out for love and comfort if that is available, as long as you are asking the other person to do it with you rather than for you. Here are some ways you can bring spiritual love and comfort into your life.

- Sit in a comfortable place or walk outside in nature.

- Listen to soothing music.

- Hold a doll or stuffed animal that represents your inner child, or look at a photo of yourself as a small child.

- Breathe into your heart and open to learning about loving yourself.

- Consciously invite Spirit in by simply saying, "I invite your love and comfort into my heart." Stay as present as you can. By practicing becoming present, you will eventually be able to feel the subtle warmth of Spirit filling you.

- Imagine that you are giving love and comfort to an actual child, and speak out loud to your inner child, saying things like, "Sweet little one, I'm here, and Spirit is here. You are not alone. I love you so much. You are such a wonderful being, and I'm so blessed and privileged to be the one to love you and take care of you."

- If you can't bring enough love and comfort into yourself due to trauma, reach out for comfort from another, but be sure that you are not handing your inner child to the other person, making that person responsible for your feelings. Be sure that you are holding your inner child while you are being held or comforted in some other way by the other person.

- Often, the best way of bringing love and comfort to yourself is to offer it to another. Giving love to another without an agenda is the surest way of feeling filled with love. The more love we share, the more full of love we feel.

I love the messages in the movie *Frozen*. When Queen Elsa accidently freezes her sister Anna's heart, Anna is told that "only an act of true love can thaw a frozen heart." Everyone assumes that this act of true love needs to come from someone else, like love's first kiss, but near the end, we discover that it needs to be expressed by Anna herself. When Anna shows her love for her sister by saving Elsa's life at the risk of her own, her own act of true love melts her heart. The other wonderful message of the movie is that fear, which is coming from Elsa's wounded self, causes her to freeze everything, and love is what thaws everything. It's so true that it's our own love for ourselves and others that brings the life back into everything.

My experience with my clients over the years has shown me that the happiest people are those who are able to love themselves and share their love, who are full of love and receive great joy from giving to others and helping others. The amount of money they have or the material things they own have little to do with their level of happiness. My wealthy clients who use their money to help others are far happier than those who hoard money out of fear.

Beginning to Manifest Your Passionate Purpose

In the last chapter, we did some work on discovering your passionate purpose. Manifesting your passionate purpose is a three-fold process:

- Have a clear vision of what you want to manifest.

- Keep your frequency high so that Spirit can manifest with you. Your Divine guidance is always here, wanting to help you manifest your dreams, but you need to be open to learning about loving yourself and keeping your body healthy, so your frequency will be high enough for Spirit to co-create with you.

- Take loving actions toward your goals, but at the same time, detach your happiness and worth from achieving your goals. If your happiness and worth are attached to the outcome, you will be trying to control, and your frequency will be too low to manifest. You need to take responsibility for making yourself happy and defining your worth intrinsically to manifest. There is a huge difference between taking loving actions toward manifesting your goals and attaching your worth and happiness to achieving your goals. The more you learn to define your intrinsic worth, the easier it will be to be unattached to outcomes. We will be doing more work on defining your worth in the next chapter, in step 5, taking loving action.

The first thing you need is a clear vision of what you want.

My vision of what I want is:

_____

_____

_____

_____

Ask your guidance, "What is the loving action I need to take now to manifest my vision?"

_____

_____

_____

_____

This is a question you need to keep asking as you move toward manifesting your vision.

If you find yourself resisting taking loving action, explore your fear. Are you afraid to fail? And if you are, what are you telling yourself that is causing this fear?

Why am I afraid of taking loving action?

_____

_____

_____

_____

What am I telling myself that is causing this fear?

_____

_____

_____

_____

We will be working much more with taking loving action, as well as with resistance to taking loving action and the resulting procrastination, in the next chapter.

Accessing Your Divine Guidance Without an Agenda

It is easiest to receive information from your guidance regarding what is in your highest good when you are feeling good and have no specific questions on your mind. This is a great time to receive creative ideas or new information about loving yourself and others. It is an open-ended inquiry with your guidance. This is how I access most of my creative ideas, as well as information regarding many aspects of self-care and about how our universe works.

Open inquiry requires moving into a state of surrender, something the wounded self hates doing. To the wounded self, surrender means losing itself and losing control over avoiding pain, while to the loving adult, it means opening the mind, heart, and soul to the love, peace, joy, and wisdom of our Divine guidance.

Until you take the risk of surrender, you won't discover that when you surrender, rather than losing control, you gain a greater degree of control over your ability to manifest your dreams. Until you surrender, you have no way of knowing that you are always being guided in your highest good.

> Ask your guidance, "What do you want to tell me right now?" and then just let go, writing or speaking aloud anything that comes through you. Don't judge it or edit it—just let it flow.
>
> _____
>
> _____
>
> _____
>
> _____
>
> _____

For me, surrender means completely relaxing and going into an almost dream-like state. In this state, I'm listening for the quiet voice of my Divine guidance, and I'm open to seeing the subtle images that my guidance brings me. Sometimes, especially when I'm working with clients, I receive 3-D images of things that have happened to them or things that are currently going on in their lives. I've found that when I'm fully open with the intent to be a channel of love for my client, I not only tap into my Divine guidance but I also tap into theirs.

The more you practice surrendering to your guidance, the more you will find yourself accessing information about what's in your highest good. It's an amazing feeling to experience that I'm never alone, that I'm always surrounded by the love, comfort, and wisdom of my guidance. I never had this experience before practicing Inner Bonding, and I know that you too will know that you are never alone as you continue to learn and practice this profound process.

Step 5

Take Loving Action

You have opened to your feelings in step 1, moved into the intent to learn about loving yourself and about truth in step 2, dialogued with your core self and your wounded self in step 3, and opened to learning about truth and loving action with your spiritual guidance in step 4. Now, in step 5, you will take the loving actions, based on truth, that you were guided to take in step 4. Over time, taking the loving action is what heals the shame, anger, aloneness, emptiness, guilt, jealousy, anxiety, and depression that have been the result of your self-abandonment.

Without taking loving action, the first four steps mean nothing. No healing will occur otherwise. Imagine that you have a son who comes to you crying because he is getting bullied at school. You listen and sympathize, but you do nothing to help the child learn to manage the bullying; nor do you go to the school and talk to the principal and teacher about the issue or call the parents of the bullies. Your son will not feel safe or loved by you without those loving actions. Yet too often, people are aware of their pain and might even tune in to what they need to do, but in the end, they ignore their Divine guidance. So let's explore anything that might be blocking you from taking loving action.

What's in the Way?

Years ago, I had my mother's angry, bullying, critical, and diminishing voice pounding away at me almost nonstop. Because my mother couldn't see her own beautiful essence, she couldn't see mine, and she projected onto me her deep feelings of inadequacy. She never went to college, and when I started college, she said to me, "Well, maybe you can finish two years and then get married and have children." Even though I had excelled in high school, she couldn't get past her own beliefs about herself to see anything about who I really was.

As a result of integrating my mother's voice into my wounded self, along with her need to diminish me due to her own deep insecurities, when my wounded self was yammering away at me, I believed that what it was saying about my limitations to act for my benefit was true. These were some of my wounded self's objections.

- "There is no point in trying to do something unless you do it perfectly."

- "Who do you think you are? What makes you think you can help others?"

- "You will never be good enough, so don't bother trying."

- "It's too scary to speak up. What if people are mad at you? If they don't like you, that proves that you are not good enough."

While I wasn't a resistant person, and procrastination was not one of my issues, this critical, controlling voice kept me too scared to take loving actions on my own behalf. Only after I was able to access my Divine guidance for the truth and risked taking loving actions based on this truth could I stop the voice of my wounded self, transform these false beliefs, and truly express who I am.

I've worked with countless people who spent years in therapy exploring their childhood and becoming aware of why they are suffering, without anything changing for them to alleviate their pain. They became good at describing their problems, and some even were able to help others, but nevertheless, they remained stuck, because they did not take loving action on their own behalf.

Jerry consulted with me because he often felt anxious and empty inside and rarely felt happy. Jerry had been a sensitive and loving child, but he had shut down his sensitivity and caring when he was around thirteen after being terrorized at school by bullies. He tried talking with his parents about it, but they did nothing to help him. He concluded that there was something wrong with him and became his own bully—harshly criticizing himself for his lack of "manliness." He decided that being a "real man" meant being like the boys who were bullying him—harsh, controlling, and insensitive. His self-judgments were ruling his life, causing him intense anxiety, aloneness, and emptiness. Through his Inner Bonding work, Jerry could see that treating himself harshly was causing his pain, yet he was so addicted to believing that this is what kept him safe that he was extremely resistant to treating himself with kindness and caring. He falsely believed that if he were kind to himself, he would be taken advantage of and hurt by others and would feel even worse than he currently felt.

Like Jerry, many people have deep resistance to taking loving actions on their own behalf due to fears and false beliefs about what will happen if they do so. We explored some of these beliefs in the last chapter, and here we will go deeper into the resistance and resulting procrastination that might be keeping you stuck.

Discovering the Root Causes of Resistance and Procrastination

Take a moment to think about the last time you procrastinated. What was happening inside you? The chances are that one part of your wounded self, which we can call the Controller, was telling you what to do with a critical, parental tone of voice:

- "It's time to get rid of this clutter."

- "You need to start getting up early and exercising."

- "Quit eating junk—you need to lose weight and get healthy."

- "You'd better get this work done on time."

- "Hurry up. You're going to be late…again."

At the same time, this same critical voice might also have been saying things like, "You'd better not make mistakes or fail. If you do, everyone will know you're stupid," or "If you fail, no one will like you. You'll be rejected, and you'll end up alone." Let's explore your own Controller voice further.

What does your inner Controller say to you?

_____

_____

_____

_____

Whom does this Controller sound like? Your mother or father? A sibling? Who else might have tried to control you and judged you for mistakes and failures when you were growing up?

_____

_____

_____

You might have been young when you integrated this Controller voice into your wounded self, even as young as two. Or you might have absorbed this critical voice when you started elementary school or secondary school. This critical voice is often an adolescent who wants to be in control—believing that if it can get you to do everything "right," you will be safe from rejection. How old were you when you integrated this voice into your wounded self?

_____

_____

There's another part of the wounded self that fosters procrastination. We can call this part the Resister, because it says, "You're not the boss of me—I don't need to do what you say" or "I'd better not even try; it's better not to try than to try and fail." Generally, the resistant part of the wounded self is younger than the controlling part.

How old were you when you started to resist? Two? Five? Ten?

_____

_____

As you become more aware of what's happening inside of you, you will see that there is likely an inner power struggle going on, with the critical part of you trying to control what you do, and the stubborn part resisting being controlled and trying to avoid the possibility of making mistakes or failing. This power struggle creates an inner immobilization, which results in procrastination. Control + resistance = procrastination. Do you really want your decisions to be determined by a child or an adolescent? Let's look more closely at your inner Resister.

What happened as you were growing up that made you so fearful of being controlled by someone? How did resisting being controlled become more important to you than loving yourself?

_____

_____

_____

_____

_____

The Resister operates from a set of false beliefs:

- "The only way I can be my own person and not lose myself is to resist."

- "Resisting control—even resisting my own Controller or my Divine guidance—is essential to my integrity and individuality."

- "My only choices when another person or my Controller are attempting to control me are to comply or to resist."

- "When someone is trying to control me, it's their fault that I resist."

- "The only way I can avoid being controlled by my Controller, by others, or by my guidance is by resisting."

What are some of your beliefs about what will happen if you stop resisting?

_____

_____

_____

_____

_____

Ask your guidance, "What is the truth about these beliefs?"

_____

_____

_____

_____

_____

Resisting won't stop others from controlling you if they want to. If someone knows that you resist being on time, they can control you by telling you a meeting time earlier than the actual time. One of my clients hated being late to social events, so she had learned to always give her husband a time the event started that was a half-hour earlier than it really was. Her husband didn't realize that he was being controlled by her.

The only time we are our own person and true to ourselves is when we neither comply nor resist but instead go inside and ask our Divine guidance, "What is in my highest good?" When someone asks me to do something in a controlling, parental voice, instead of just complying or resisting, I go inside and say, "Is it loving to me to do what this person wants or not? Is it in my highest good and the highest good of the other person?" I am true to myself and my own person when I do what is in my highest good.

The same holds true for moments when you resist yourself, your Controller voice. You will be able to take loving action when you don't automatically resist your Controller but instead open to learning about what is loving to you. When loving yourself has a higher priority than resisting being controlled by your own Controller or by another person—or by your false belief that your guidance will try to control you—you will be able to resolve your addictions to resistance and procrastination.

In which of the six main areas of life are you resisting and procrastinating? In what areas are you stuck in not taking loving action?

Emotional: Yes _____   No _____

Physical: Yes _____   No _____

Financial: Yes _____   No _____

Relationships: Yes _____   No _____

Organizational: Yes _____   No _____

Spiritual: Yes _____   No _____

What does the controlling, critical voice of your wounded self say to you regarding these areas of procrastination?

_____

_____

_____

_____

_____

What does the resistant part of your wounded self say or do in response to the controlling voice?

_____

_____

_____

_____

What do you feel inside when this power struggle is going on within? What do you feel when you resist and procrastinate?

_____

_____

_____

_____

What do you feel inside when you receive guidance regarding what is loving to you, but you resist to not be controlled by your guidance?

_____

_____

_____

_____

Sometimes you might resist because doing hard things feels lonely to you. When this is the case, you need to ask someone to join you. When I was moving out of my house, which I lived in for thirty-one years, the thought of cleaning out the attic made me feel lonely, so I always made sure I had someone helping me. One of my clients, an author, found that she didn't procrastinate writing when she wrote in an Internet café with people around her. She didn't need to speak with them—she just didn't want to be alone.

After I wrote an article on procrastination, I received the following email:

I always want to do hard things with or in the company of other people, and I've always considered myself bad for this, and my family makes fun of me for it. What a joy to read your post and find out being in company helps alleviate procrastination!

Moving Out of Procrastination

Imagine that you have two board games. One game is played by the various aspects and ages of your wounded self, with the intent to control and not be controlled and to protect against mistakes, failure, and rejection. The other game is played by a loving adult, whose intent is to be loving to you and to others.

The way out of procrastination is to change board games, which, of course, you do by changing your intent from controlling to loving. As long as your intent is to protect, avoid, control, and not be controlled, you will remain stuck in resistance. When you choose the intent to learn about what is loving to you and to others, and when being loving with yourself and others is your highest priority, you will get unstuck.

When your intent is to love yourself, rather than letting your fear of failure, rejection, or being controlled consume you, you will find it easy to take loving actions on your own behalf.

This is when it becomes easy to get your house clean, to eat well and exercise, to get things done on time and get places on time—because this is what is loving to you.

Sometimes, before you can shift your intent, you need to consciously choose to resist as a way of becoming more aware of it.

The next time you find yourself resisting and procrastinating doing something, make a choice to consciously resist. Do it on purpose rather than just letting these aspects of your wounded self take over. Consciously say, "No, I'm not going to be loving to myself by doing this." How does it feel to resist on purpose?

_____

_____

_____

_____

The more you consciously choose to resist and procrastinate, the more the choice to take loving action becomes available to you, because you become aware that you are actually making a choice to resist. When you resist automatically, it doesn't seem that you have a choice, even though you are the one choosing your intent. It's when you become aware of *choosing* to resist, rather than automatically resisting, that you can then choose to take loving action. Choosing to resist can also help you tune in to what you really want and what is in your highest good.

Ask your inner child, "How would you feel if, rather than just resist, I checked in with what you really want and checked with Divine guidance regarding what is in my highest good?"

_____

_____

_____

_____

Moving Beyond Perfectionism

Do you have an aspect of your wounded self who believes that if you were perfect, you could have control over how others feel about you and treat you? I used to believe this, and it certainly made my life hard. If this is an issue for you, this exercise might help.

Ask your wounded self, "What does 'perfect' mean to you?"

_____

_____

_____

_____

Ask your wounded self, "Where did you get this concept of perfection? What happened as we were growing up that led to this concept of perfect?"

_____

_____

_____

_____

Ask your wounded self, "What happened as we were growing up that led you to believe that you could have control over others by being perfect?"

_____

_____

_____

_____

Ask your wounded self, "What makes you believe that you can know what another person's concept of perfection is?"

_____

_____

_____

_____

Your wounded self is incapable of understanding that each person has their own ideas of what "perfection" means and also that your soul essence is *already perfect*. Since it's a spark of the Divine, how could it not be perfect? The more you get to know the beauty of your soul, the easier it will be for you to let go of worrying about being perfect and of allowing your fears of not being perfect to get in the way of taking loving actions.

Fear of Failure

If you are not taking loving action because of a fear of failure, there are false beliefs you absorbed as you were growing up that are fueling this fear. Here is an exercise you can do to help you move beyond the fear of failure or beyond allowing your fear to stop you from taking loving action.

What were you told about failure as you were growing up—or what was your experience of failure—that may have created a fear of failure?

_____

_____

_____

_____

Fear of failure is entwined with the consequences that might result if we do fail. Your wounded self may attribute meaning to failure. For example, your wounded self might say that if you fail, you are a failure as a person or you will have made a fool of yourself. Or do you tell yourself that if you fail, everyone who thought you were smart will now think you are stupid? Tune in to what you tell yourself that may be keeping you stuck in not taking loving action.

> **What does your wounded self currently tell you about what failure means?**
>
> _____
>
> _____
>
> _____
>
> _____
>
> _____
>
> **Open to learning with your Divine guidance and ask for the truth about failure. Write down whatever comes to you.**
>
> _____
>
> _____
>
> _____
>
> _____

The loving adult knows that failure is a part of life, that it offers us valuable lessons, that it has nothing to do with your worth as a person, and that most successful people have had numerous failures. I love what Edison said as he was inventing the light bulb: "I have not failed. I've just found ten thousand ways that won't work," and "I am not discouraged, because every wrong attempt discarded is another step forward."

> If a fear of failure is keeping you from taking loving action, ask your Divine guidance, "What do I need to do to get over the fear of failure? What loving action can I take that will start to help heal this fear?"
>
> _____
>
> _____
>
> _____
>
> _____

What I've done that has completely healed my fear of failure is I've told my inner child, "It's okay to make mistakes or to fail. I will still love you if you fail." Because my inner child knows that my love for her is based on my intrinsic qualities and not on my performance, she no longer fears my judgment of her if we fail. This has freed me to take many risks that I would never have previously taken.

False Beliefs About Selfishness

There is a common false belief that taking loving care of yourself makes you self-centered—that being loving means denying your own feelings and sacrificing yourself to caretake others. This false belief can keep you from taking loving action for yourself at the cost of abandoning your inner child. When other people affirm this belief, because they are takers and expect you to sacrifice yourself for them to prove your love, you will experience a vicious cycle of reinforcement for giving yourself up.

> What is your wounded self's definition of selfish?
>
> _____
>
> _____
>
> _____

How does this definition of selfishness cause you to abandon yourself?

_____

_____

_____

How does it prevent you from taking loving action for yourself?

_____

_____

_____

Since we can't turn to others to model the loving actions we need to take for our own well-being, we need to turn to Divine guidance to learn. When I asked my Divine guidance the definition of selfishness, here are the answers that came through.

We are being selfish when

- we consider only ourselves and don't consider the effect our behavior has on others,

- we expect others to give themselves up and do what we want them to do, rather than do what brings them joy or is in their highest good,

- we keep drawing a conversation back to ourselves rather than listening to and caring about what another is saying,

- we punish others when they think and feel differently than we do, and

- we harm others for our own ends.

It's important for you to define selfishness for yourself with the help of your Divine guidance and to learn about when you are being selfish.

Ask your Divine guidance, "What is the definition of selfishness? What am I doing when I am selfish?"

_____

_____

_____

_____

Loving yourself and taking loving actions on your own behalf is self-responsible and in your highest good. It's not selfish! You are being self-responsible and loving yourself when

- you do what brings you joy with no intent to harm another, even if another person doesn't like it;

- you support your own highest good, even when someone wants you to do something other than what you are doing;

- you support others in doing what is in their highest good and what brings them joy, even if it's not what you want;

- you are considerate of others' wants and needs without giving yourself up; and

- you speak your truth without blame or judgment.

Your loving connection to your inner child and to your Divine guidance can break the cycle of others reinforcing your false belief that you are being selfish when you take loving care of yourself. As you deepen your Inner Bonding practice, clarity about what is good for yourself will strengthen your resolve amid other people's requests and even their demands. This resolve will support taking the loving actions you identified in step 4.

Taking Loving Actions—Burden or Freedom

When I was growing up, I always got the feeling that my needs were a burden to my mother. Being a sickly child with asthma, I would often wake up in the night unable to breathe. Even though my mother didn't work and had plenty of time to nap during the day if she didn't get a good night's sleep, she was generally annoyed about having to take care of me at night. In fact, she was annoyed by anything other than me acting like I was fine. So, of course, I learned to act like I was fine most of the time.

Does your wounded self believe that taking loving actions on your own behalf is a bother and a burden? That it's too hard, and that it's easier to try to get someone else to do it? While this is true if you are operating as a child or adolescent wounded self, it's definitely not at all true for the loving adult. For example, if you have a hungry, crying baby, would it be easier to go knocking on doors, asking if someone would feed the baby, or would it be easier to nurse the baby or give the baby a bottle? Of course it would be easier to feed the baby yourself. The same is true of taking loving care of yourself.

Do you believe that taking loving actions on your own behalf is a burden? If you do, why do you believe this? Where does this belief come from? Write down what happened as you were growing up that led to you conclude this.

_____

_____

_____

_____

_____

_____

Do you believe that you will feel worthy and loved if someone else takes responsibility for your feelings and needs and that it means more if someone else does it than if you do it? If you believe this, where did you get this belief?

_____

_____

_____

_____

Do you believe that someone else should do it for you now because no one did it as you were growing up? Do you believe that it's easier to try to have control over getting someone else to love you than to be loving to yourself? If you do, where did you get these beliefs?

_____

_____

_____

_____

Do you believe that someone else can care for you better than you can? That someone else can know what you want and need better than you can? If you do, where did you get this belief?

_____

_____

_____

_____

Do you believe that it takes too much time and energy to take loving care of yourself? If you do, where did you get this belief?

_____

_____

How much time and energy have you spent in your life trying to get others' love, acceptance, attention, and approval? Describe some of the situations you have found yourself in as a result.

_____

_____

_____

Has trying to get someone else to do these things led to you feeling safe, secure, peaceful, and worthy? What has been the result of trying to get someone else to love you?

_____

_____

_____

_____

The truth we all need to face is that even if someone else is loving you and giving you what you've always wanted, if you are abandoning yourself, you won't feel safe, worthy, and lovable. If you had a child whom you kept trying to give away to someone else to love, that child would always feel rejected by you, even if another person was loving to him or her. You can't reject and abandon yourself without feeling anxious, depressed, unworthy, unlovable, empty, alone, and angry. No one can do for you what you need to do for yourself. The love that others give you feels great, but it needs to be the icing on the cake, not the cake itself. Once you provide the cake—by loving yourself—others' love is wonderful, but if you are rejecting and abandoning yourself, there is nowhere for the icing to go. Your love for yourself provides the foundation for others' love.

> Joleen's mother passed away when she was eighteen months old. At that time, her relatives were told by well-meaning doctors and professionals that it would not affect her, because she wouldn't remember her mother, which turned out not to be true at all. The trauma and inattention to the issues she had due to this huge loss, combined with her high sensitivity and a dad and stepmom who were self-abandoning, made childhood quite a challenge for Joleen. She developed severe anxiety and depression, which she learned to escape from by disconnecting from her feelings and focusing in her head.
>
> Joleen believed that once she could get away from home and be on her own, things would change. But they didn't change, because she kept looking outside of herself for the source of all her pain, and she kept trying to control everything external to her. There was still a little girl inside of her that wasn't being heard, and she had no idea how to take care of herself.
>
> As Joleen developed her loving adult and learned to love herself, her anxiety and depression gradually healed. Because she was no longer treating herself the way her parents had treated her, she was no longer pulling on her husband for love, and so her marriage, as well as her relationship with her children, greatly improved.

Now it's time for action—loving action! One of the first and most important loving actions you can take is learning to define your own intrinsic worth.

Defining Your Intrinsic Worth

In step 3, when learning about your inner child, you started to see your essence through the eyes of your Divine guidance. Now we will go deeper into defining your own worth, because this is *very* important. We take loving care of what we value, so learning to value your true self is vital to being motivated to love yourself and take loving action on your own behalf.

Imagine that you have a baby or you adopt a baby. What makes the baby worthy of love?

_____

_____

_____

_____

Picture yourself as a baby, or actually look at a photo of yourself as a baby. Are you, as a baby, deserving of love? If you are, why?

_____

_____

_____

_____

Now picture yourself as a small child, or look at a photo of yourself as a child. Let yourself go inside and remember what you were like as a small child. What were you like before your wounded self took over? Extrovert or introvert, outgoing or shy? Caring? Empathic? Sensitive? Highly energetic? Funny? Creative? Affectionate? What is your unique spark of the Divine? What are your special gifts and talents? Try to come up with words that describe you as a little child. If you had a child who was exactly like you were as a child, what would you love about the child? How would you describe the child to someone else?

_____

_____

_____

_____

_____

_____

_____

Is there anything about you as a child that doesn't deserve love?

_____

_____

As you did in step 3, visualize your Divine guidance. Ask your guidance to give you more information about who you are as a soul. Write down what you receive in response.

_____

_____

_____

_____

_____

I encourage you to keep asking your guidance for information about your true soul self. Over time, you will come to love and value the magnificence of your soul. This is when it becomes easy to take loving care of yourself.

If your parents or caregivers couldn't see their own essence, they couldn't see yours, so you might not have received the love you needed. Now, as a loving adult, you have a chance to give your inner child the love you might never have received as you were growing up.

Loving parents mirror their children's beautiful qualities. One way of giving love to your inner child is to mirror your beautiful qualities, such as saying, "Thank you for your kindness toward that person" or "I so appreciate your creativity" or "I love your laughter" or "I love your sense of humor." What are some of the wonderful qualities of your soul essence that you can mirror right now? What can you appreciate about your soul right now?

_____

_____

_____

_____

_____

It's great to get into the habit of mirroring your essence throughout the day. I do this all day long and out loud—unless there are others around. Whenever I do something that I value, I tell my inner child how much I appreciate her and that I feel privileged to be the one to take loving care of her.

Of course, it's not enough to just define your own worth. For your inner child to feel loved and valued by you, you need to treat him or her as you would treat someone you valued. Your inner child will not feel loved by you if you keep abandoning yourself. Barbara, normally a gentle person, had gotten angry at a friend of hers. Afterward—mortified—she explored her anger.

ADULT BARBARA: Little one, why were you so angry at Angie?

CHILD BARBARA: I'm sick and tired of you constantly giving to Angie, but when I needed help, she wasn't there. You're always giving and giving to everyone, and then you just allow everyone to take and take from us. I'm so tired of you always taking responsibility for everything and everyone else other than me.

ADULT BARBARA: How do you feel when I value other people's needs and not yours?

CHILD BARBARA: Completely and utterly worthless—and you constantly remind me of this. You tell me that my needs don't matter and that everything would just be so much easier if I were just quiet.

ADULT BARBARA (to wounded self):   Why do you give to others but ignore our own feelings and needs?

WOUNDED SELF: Because I need approval and validation. I don't want anyone thinking that I'm a bad and horrible person. I can't deal with the pain of someone not liking me. I don't get attention from you, so need to get it from somewhere.

ADULT BARBARA (to inner child):   So it's not really Angie you're angry at—it's me. Is that right?

CHILD BARBARA: Yes. I felt that if I weren't really angry, you wouldn't notice me, as I'm nothing to you. I was terrified that again you would make Angie more valued and important than me. I needed to be sure to come in stronger and harder, seeing as you never choose me.

ADULT BARBARA (to Divine guidance):   What can I do to make this better?

DIVINE GUIDANCE   Commit to giving your inner child at least as much attention as you give to others. Connect with her throughout the day. Make loving her your priority.

Barbara could mirror her inner child and tell her all day how wonderful she is, but if she continued to ignore her and make everyone else more important than her, she would continue to feel worthless. Defining your worth *and* taking the loving action you would take for someone you value is what eventually creates a deep sense of self-worth.

Loving Actions in the Six Major Areas of Life

Go back to the last step, step 4, to the section called "Loving Actions in the Six Major Areas of Self-Responsibility," and review what loving actions your guidance advised you to take emotionally, physically, financially, relationally, organizationally, and spiritually. Write those loving actions in each area below, and then pick one or two that you will take right now.

Emotional loving actions advised by my guidance:

_____

_____

_____

_____

The action I will take starting now is:

_____

_____

_____

_____

Physical loving actions advised by my guidance:

_____

_____

_____

The action I will take starting now is:

_____

_____

_____

_____

Financial loving actions advised by my guidance:

_____

_____

_____

_____

The action I will take starting now is:

_____

_____

_____

_____

Relationship loving actions advised by my guidance:

_____

_____

_____

_____

The action I will take starting now is:

_____

_____

_____

_____

Organizational loving actions advised by my guidance:

_____

_____

_____

_____

The action I will take starting now is:

_____

_____

_____

_____

Spiritual loving actions advised by my guidance:

_____

_____

_____

_____

The action I will take starting now is:

_____

_____

You can start with one loving action and gradually build into taking the other actions advised by your Divine guidance. This is an ongoing process, since new situations always come up in life in which we need to take loving actions on our own behalf or on behalf of others. With time and practice, you can ask your Divine guidance in any given moment, "What is the loving action right now?" and receive an answer.

Clients often ask me, "When will I get there?" To them, "getting there" means that they will feel happy and fulfilled all the time. I used to believe the same thing—that I would reach a point where I always understood what loving actions to take and would always feel great as a result—but now I know that life will always present me with new situations in which to learn and grow. I now know that what worked for me previously might not work later, even if the situation is similar. I've accepted that it's always going to be a process and that there is no such thing as "getting there."

Clients also ask me, "Should I always do what my inner child wants?" If you are a parent, do you always do what your children want? Of course not! As I stated in step 3, in the discussion about the wounded self, it's the wounded self that is authoritarian or permissive. If your inner child wants ice cream for breakfast, allowing that would be self-indulgent. On the other hand, if you never let yourself eat ice cream or other favorite treats, you might be behaving from your authoritarian wounded self, setting limits that are too rigid.

Rather than allowing the authoritarian or permissive wounded self to make the decisions or allowing everything your inner child wants, check in with your Divine guidance to see if it's in your highest good. When it comes to taking action for your inner child, it is always important to ask your Divine guidance, "What is the loving action right now? What is in my highest good right now?" These questions were the key to unlocking Lynette's joy and freedom in life.

Lynette consulted with me because she often felt scared and alone and had no idea what to do with these feelings. She didn't know how to pay attention to and learn from her painful feelings or how to give love to her inner child. The concept of taking loving care of her own feelings and needs was foreign to her. Instead, she would overwhelm a close friend with her issues, believing that others or external circumstances were the cause of how she felt. If her friend wasn't available, she would sleep, eat, go out to bars, or go shopping to distract herself.

When Lynette discovered that she not only had the right to take loving care of herself but also that it was actually her responsibility to do so, she dived into the practice. She was amazed at the peace and joy she felt when she learned to be compassionate with herself and present with her painful feelings rather than trying to get someone else to take care of them. She loved receiving the deeper wisdom, understanding, and peace from her spiritual guidance that supported her in lovingly managing her emotions and that helped her to be compassionate rather than needy with her friends and family. She loved that she no longer felt like a victim of others and of life.

The Joy and Freedom of Taking Loving Actions

Dorothy, in *The Wizard of Oz*, was able to be a loving adult and take much loving action for herself throughout the movie, in spite of being so young. Her kindness to the Scarecrow, the Cowardly Lion, and the Tin Man, who represented aspects of her essence—intelligence, courage, and heart—enabled her to melt the Wicked Witch of the West, who was one aspect of the wounded self. She also exposed the Wizard—another aspect of the wounded self. This led to the Good Witch of the North—her higher guidance—finally showing her how to get home, where she experienced the joy of reconnection. Can you similarly begin to imagine the joy and personal power that you might feel at having the freedom to take loving actions on your own behalf?

Use your imagination and make up a story about how much joy and personal power you might feel at giving yourself the complete freedom to take loving actions on your behalf and on behalf of others.

_____

_____

_____

_____

_____

_____

_____

_____

Evaluating Your Actions

In the long run, the result of taking loving actions will be a deep sense of inner peace and fullness.

The biggest addiction I had was to caretaking. I had been trained by both my mother and my grandmother to sacrifice myself for others, and doing this felt like survival to me. I continued this addiction in my marriage and with my children—always concerned with their feelings and ignoring my own. The result of this was that by the time I was in my mid-forties, I was quite ill. I saw various doctors to try to discover what was wrong. I was told that my immune system wasn't functioning well and that I was on my way to a serious illness, such as cancer. I have no doubt that had I continued on the path I was on, even though I was eating well, I would not be alive today.

Being a sensitive person, I easily absorbed others' feelings, and I could feel my husband's and children's feelings even when I was in another part of the house or even not in the house. As I pulled away from taking responsibility for their feelings, they became angry with me, which has always been hard for me. Growing up with a mother who frequently raged at me, and never learning how to take care of my feelings in the face of her rage, I froze like a deer in the headlights when someone was angry with me—especially someone I loved.

While I was learning Inner Bonding and healing my addiction to caretaking, I used to sit in my art studio, which was on the third floor of our house, holding my knees and rocking back and forth, saying out loud, "I can handle this. I can handle this." My wounded self wanted more than anything to go downstairs and give them what they wanted so they wouldn't be angry with me. One of my biggest fears in taking loving care of myself, instead of everyone else, was that I would find out that they didn't love me—that their "love" was dependent upon my caretaking them. And, in fact, this is exactly what happened. My husband and I divorced, my adolescent children were distant from me, and my parents were furious with me. A fractured family was the last thing I wanted. Unbeknownst to me, my parents disowned me, which I didn't find out about until after my mother died. Fortunately, I was able to reconcile with my father before he died. I have since forgiven my parents. They did the best they could.

Yet, with all these challenges, I knew I had to do this. I had clearly heard my inner child screaming at me, *When is it my turn? When are you going to pay attention to me instead of ignoring me and judging me? When are you going to give to me what you give to everyone else? I can't live like this any longer!*

I made the hardest decision I had ever made in my life. I decided that I would rather lose everyone else than go on losing myself. That I would rather end up alone than continue to sacrifice myself and likely die.

This was a life-saving decision for me. From the time I decided this and started to take loving care of myself, my health suddenly improved. My fatigue left, and I again had energy. I felt something inside come alive, and for the first time in my life, I felt joy! And not only joy, but also a sense of freedom that I had never known.

Letting go of trying to control others into loving me with my caretaking has been the hardest and most wonderful thing I've ever done. Instead of anxiety, I now have peace. Instead of feeling flawed, I now feel whole. Instead of tiredness, I have boundless energy. Instead of feeling lost, I always feel guided, and I never feel alone.

Currently, my ex-husband and I are friends, and, while there are still some rocky times, I'm now closer with my children and grandchildren. The results of my loving actions were hugely challenging in the short run, but in the long run, I will be forever grateful that I made the unwavering choice to love myself.

How You Feel After Taking Loving Action

Your feelings, which are your inner guidance, tell you whether or not the action you took was loving to you. When we take an action that is truly loving to ourselves, we generally feel a sense of relief, along with other positive feelings.

In the last chapter, you wrote down the loving actions that you were going to take, and hopefully you took at least one of them, or you imagined taking the action. Write down the loving action you took or imagined taking:

_____

_____

_____

_____

Mindfully breathe back into your body, as you did in step 1, getting present in your body with your feelings. What do you feel as a result of taking the loving action?

_____

_____

_____

_____

If you are not feeling some relief and a lightening of your energy, and if you are not feeling more peace and fullness inside, you may need to go back to step 4 and ask your Divine guidance for another loving action. Loving actions always bring some positive results, although they might not be immediately apparent.

Some loving actions won't feel *good*, but they will feel *right* inside. When you are evaluating your loving action, you may need to focus on the long-term results, not the momentary results. Some loving actions, such as stopping smoking or giving up sugar or alcohol or some other addiction, generally feel awful in the short term, but they may feel great in the long term. Giving up caretaking might feel scary at first but will be empowering later. Speaking your truth to someone close to you might result in that person being angry with you, but in the long run, it might result in him or her respecting you.

If your loving action doesn't feel good, does it feel right? Tune inside and ask your inner child, "Does my loving action feel right?"

_____

_____

_____

In the long run, loving actions heal false beliefs. Is there a belief that you challenged by taking the loving action you took? If so, what was the belief and what do you now know to be true? For example, if you've believed that you need to judge yourself to get yourself to do things right, and you gave yourself compassion rather than judgment, what happened? Write down the belief and what you now know to be true.

- Belief: _____

_____

- Loving action: _____

_____

- What I now know to be true: _____

_____

You can tell yourself all day that you are a wonderful, beautiful soul, but if you don't take loving action on your own behalf, you inner child won't believe you. With actual children, telling them how wonderful they are, but then ignoring them, judging them, shutting them out with your addictions, or trying to make others responsible for them will leave them feeling abandoned and rejected by you. The same holds true for your inner child.

Your inner child feels loved, valued, and important to you when you take loving actions on your behalf. The more loving action you take, the more your sense of self-worth and personal power will soar and the more joy you will feel in your life. Again, think about the loving action you took, and ask your inner child the following questions:

"Does the action I took make you feel safer inside and more empowered? If so, how? If not, why not?"

_____

_____

_____

_____

"Does the action I took make you feel more loved by me and more important to me? If so, how? If not, why not? Did I hear you accurately? If not, what didn't I hear accurately?"

_____

_____

_____

_____

"Does the action I took make you feel less alone? Does it make you feel that I have your back? If not, why not?"

_____

_____

_____

_____

"Do you feel fuller inside as a result of the action I took? If not, why not?"

_____

_____

_____

_____

"Does the action I took make you feel lighter, with a higher frequency? If not, why not?"

_____

_____

_____

_____

"Is there some other action you want me to take right now?"

_____

_____

_____

_____

If your pain, anger, shame, or other wounded feelings are not lessening, and your inner child doesn't know what action he or she wants, then go back to step 4, connecting with your Divine guidance, to discover another loving action. Be assured that when you take loving actions on your own behalf, life will eventually feel better.

Making Your Best Right Decisions

Decisions become much easier to make when you are focused on what is loving to you. Decisions, especially important ones, are frequently difficult for many people. Do you often go back and forth, trying to figure out the right thing to do? I used to do that, but not anymore. Now I make decisions quickly, and I'm generally happy with the results.

Think about a situation in which you want to make a decision. It can be about anything—what new couch to get, how to spend your weekend, what to order in a restaurant, or where to go for a vacation. You can start with a simple decision or use a more complex, life-changing decision that you are struggling over. What is the decision you are struggling over? What are the options regarding this decision?

_____

_____

_____

_____

For a whole day, imagine that you pick one of the options and notice how you feel. Ask your Divine guidance if this option supports your highest good. Write how you feel and what your guidance says about this option.

_____

_____

_____

_____

The next day, imagine the other option. Again, notice how you feel and ask your Divine guidance if this option supports your highest good. Write how you feel and what your guidance says about this option.

_____

_____

_____

_____

If there are more than two options, spend a day imagining each one.

When what you feel inside agrees with what your Divine guidance is telling you, you have your decision. You want to get the feeling of everything lining up inside. It's a peaceful feeling.

Write about the option that feels peaceful inside and that your inner child and Divine guidance agree on.

_____

_____

_____

If you do this each time you have a decision to make, this will support you in trusting your feelings and your Divine guidance. You will find that you can make decisions quickly and that things in your life flow and become easier.

Glenda was struggling to make a decision between either going on a retreat that she had always dreamed of and that had the potential of opening some things up in her business, but which was quite costly, or heading up a conference that she had been asked to lead and which would be lucrative for her. I asked her to go inside and ask her inner child how she felt about going on the retreat.

Glenda's inner child said, "The thought of going on the retreat feels exciting to me. It's something I've always wanted to do. I feel open and expansive inside when I think of doing this."

Then I asked her to go inside and see how her inner child feels when she thinks of leading the conference.

Glenda's inner child said, "I like leading this kind of conference, and I would look forward to seeing many people that I know, but I also feel a sense of obligation. I know they really want me to do this, and it's hard for me to say no."

Then I asked Glenda to ask her Divine guidance which choice is in her higher good.

Glenda's Divine guidance said, "I've been encouraging you to open your work up to new areas that would be creative and exciting. Leading the conference is more of the same, but the possibilities that could open to you in going to the retreat would support moving forward in your work."

Glenda had been struggling with this decision for a week, and once she tuned in to her feelings and her guidance, it became apparent to her that going on the retreat was what she really wanted and is what was in her highest good. She breathed a sigh of relief.

Gaining Trust in Your Divine Guidance

It takes time and practice before you will fully trust your Divine guidance to the point where you are consistently willing to take the loving actions that are offered. Part of the practice is consciously testing it. When I was first connecting with my guidance, I felt like I was making it all up. So I had to test it out—over and over, even over mundane things that my guidance was reminding me of. Sometimes I would listen and consciously do what I was guided to do, and at other times, I consciously didn't do it. Invariably, things turned out better when I listened and took the loving action as a loving adult than when I didn't listen to my guidance and didn't take the advised action.

Start to notice big and little things popping into your mind. If you have a thought like *I forgot something at work*, or *I'd better call my friend*, choose to attend to it, take the loving action, and notice what happens.

What happened when I listened to my guidance was:

_____

_____

_____

_____

The next time you get a nudge from your guidance, choose to ignore it and see what happens.

What happened when I ignored my guidance was:

_____

_____

_____

_____

Keep doing this over and over, sometimes listening and taking the action, and other times ignoring your Divine guidance. It took me many tests before I started to trust my Divine guidance. Now the communication with my Divine guidance flows easily, presenting primarily as gut feelings, thoughts, intuition, or images.

Think back to some times when you had a thought or intuition about something and you didn't follow it. What happened?

_____

_____

_____

_____

Think about a time when you had an important thought or intuition and you followed it. What happened?

_____

_____

_____

_____

Being tuned in to Divine guidance, in whatever form it comes, can have huge consequences. It is a resource well worth cultivating, because in addition to increasing your experiences of joy and freedom, it can mean the difference between life and death. I recently read a story about a man whose teenage son was missing overnight. He went to the police, and they dismissed him, saying that his son might have run away. This man trusted his intuition and hired a helicopter. He spotted his son's wrecked car. His son was trapped inside with broken bones and other contusions, but he was alive after being trapped for thirty hours. Trusting his intuition, the father saved his son's life.

Access Guidance Throughout the Day

You don't need to have a problem to connect with your guidance. With enough practice, you can learn to be connected all day. Knowing that my guidance is always watching out for me brings me a deep sense of peace and safety. I love being able to turn to my guidance for what is loving to me whenever I want, and I love knowing that my guidance will get my attention if there is something important I need to attend to. My guidance has not only saved my life more than once but also consistently guides me in what is most loving to me.

I _learned_ to do this, and so can you. Before practicing Inner Bonding, I had no idea how to connect with my guidance whenever I wanted to. I never had at-will Divine connection until I learned to stay open to learning about loving myself (and I had already been taking good care of myself for a long time—by eating really well, for instance) and I learned to trust my guidance and take the advised loving actions.

While you are on a walk or sitting in a comfortable place, preferably out in nature, take some deep, mindful breaths. Consciously choose the intent to learn about loving yourself. Breathe into your heart and ask, out loud or in writing, "What is in my highest good right now?" and "What is loving to me right now?" Let go of the need to get "right" answers, and notice what pops into your mind. Say whatever comes to mind out loud, or write it down, if you are sitting down.

_____

_____

_____

_____

If nothing becomes clear, let that be okay. Just continue to stay open to thoughts, images, and feelings that feel right inside. As you continue to practice the six steps, accessing your Divine guidance will become much easier.

Practice doing this numerous times throughout the day until asking these questions becomes a new habit. You want to create new neural pathways in your brain for asking your Divine guidance these questions throughout the day. Ask it about everything, no matter how mundane it seems.

Putting It All Together

The six steps of Inner Bonding flow from one to the other. Some issues take weeks or even months to resolve, but with others, you can learn to do the whole process on the spot, within a minute or so.

The key to the process is to learn to stay in tune with your feelings all the time, as you learned to do in step 1. This way, you are alerted the moment you feel anything other than peace inside. As soon as you feel anything less than peace and fullness within, do the Inner Bonding process in any form you can. When you want to be a loving parent with a baby, you attend immediately to the baby's cry. You do the same thing with your inner child. If you are at work, perhaps you can go to the bathroom to do the process. If you are dealing with small children and can't do it right away, just make a note to do it when you can.

When you do an Inner Bonding exploration, start with what you are feeling right now or with what you feel about a particular issue or with what you feel about a past situation. Before doing the dialogue, decide if you are addressing your current feelings, your feelings about an issue, or your feelings about something in the past. Then clearly identify the topic.

What I want to address in this dialogue is:

_____

_____

Step 1

Choose to be mindful of your feelings, attending to your feelings with the willingness to feel your pain, learn about it, take responsibility for how you may be causing your pain, and realize you are responsible for creating your peace and joy.

Breathe deeply, following your breath and letting it bring you inside your body. Tune in to your body sensations. Move toward your feelings, welcoming and embracing them with compassion.

The loving adult asks the inner child, "What are you feeling right now about [the topic of the dialogue]?"

_____

_____

Make a decision that you are willing to take responsibility for your current or past feelings.

Once you are aware of how you feel and you have decided you want responsibility for your feelings, move on to step 2.

Step 2

Consciously choose the intent to learn about truth and about loving yourself, which opens the heart, and invite the wisdom, love, and compassion of Divine guidance into your heart. This is what creates the loving adult.

> Move into compassionate curiosity about what you may be thinking, doing, or not doing that is causing wounded pain. Compassionately embrace any current or past pain of life, and open to what would bring joy and peace.
>
> If anger is in the way of opening to learning, do the Anger Process from step 2 out loud or in writing. First express your anger at someone in the present, then at whomever this person reminds you of in the past. Then allow your inner child to express his or her anger at you for any way you are not taking loving care of yourself or any way you are behaving like the person you are currently angry with.
>
> You can know you are open and have the intent to learn when
>
> - your heart is filled with warmth, love, and compassion for both your wounded self and core self;
>
> - you are filled with a deep desire to know how you may be causing your pain and what you need to do to bring joy; and
>
> - you are filled with curiosity about the good reasons you have for feeling and behaving the way you are.

Once you feel open to learning, move on to step 3.

Step 3

Choose to welcome and learn with your inner child and your wounded self by dialoguing with the feelings of your inner child and the beliefs of your wounded self. With love, compassion, and curiosity, explore your feelings, behaviors, false beliefs, and memories.

Exploring Wounded Feelings and False Beliefs

As a loving adult, with kindness, gentleness, and compassion, explore what you are telling yourself and how you are treating yourself that is causing wounded feelings.

The loving adult asks the inner child, "What am I telling you, doing, or not doing, when I'm operating as the wounded self, that is causing your wounded feelings?"

_____

_____

_____

_____

The loving adult asks the wounded self, "There must be a good reason why you are treating the inner child in ways that are causing pain. What do you believe is causing this behavior? What are you trying to control or avoid feeling?"

_____

_____

_____

The loving adult asks the wounded self, "What is the fear of feeling the deeper pain of life that you might be avoiding with your protective or controlling behavior?"

_____

_____

_____

The loving adult asks the wounded self, "Where did you get these beliefs?" Open to new memories coming from within.

_____

_____

_____

_____

With kindness and compassion toward all your feelings, continue to dialogue until you reach clarity about the source of your pain.

Attending to and Learning from the Painful Feelings of Life

When there are painful life feelings—such as loneliness, heartbreak, helplessness concerning others, grief, or outrage over injustice—open to these feelings with compassion, gentleness, and tenderness so you can learn from them.

Put your hands on your heart and stay present with the feelings. Ask your inner child, "What are you telling me about a person or situation with these painful feelings?"

_____

_____

_____

Continue breathing into these feelings, holding them with deep caring and gentleness as you listen to what your inner child needs to say. When the feelings release, ask your Divine guidance to take them and replace them with peace and acceptance.

Exploring What You Want and What Brings You Joy

You can explore your desires, passions, and talents that want to be expressed, as well as what you would like to be doing regarding work and free time, any time you feel open and connected with your feelings and your guidance.

The loving adult asks the inner child questions such as, "What do you want to do this weekend?" "What would be fun to do right now?" "What would bring you joy right now?" "Who do you want to spend time with?" "How do you want to express your creativity?" Then listen openly to how he or she responds.

_____

_____

_____

_____

_____

You will know you're ready for step 4 when one of three things occurs.

- You understand how you are treating yourself that may be causing your wounded pain, and you are aware of the false beliefs fueling your self-abandoning behavior.

- You have lovingly managed the deeper pain of life and opened to learning with your inner child about any other information your inner child wants to tell you about a person or situation.

- You have openly heard what your inner child wants and what may bring you joy.

Step 4

Use your imagination to dialogue with your Divine guidance.

Dialogue Regarding Truth and Loving Action

Accessing the truth from your Divine guidance is an essential aspect, along with taking loving action based on the truth, for healing false beliefs.

Imagining your Divine guidance, ask, "What is the truth about these beliefs?" Let go and allow your guidance to write or speak through you about any of the beliefs you uncovered in step 3.

_____

_____

_____

_____

_____

Once you get a sense of the truth, bring the truth inside to your wounded self and your inner child. Ask your Divine guidance, "What is the loving action toward my inner child? What is in my highest good?" Open and allow your guidance to answer through you.

_____

_____

_____

_____

_____

_____

Dialogue Regarding the Existential Pain of Life

Your Divine guidance can help you learn to lovingly manage the existential pain of life, which can help prevent these painful feelings from becoming stuck in your body.

Ask your Divine guidance, "What do you want to tell me about the person or situation that is causing or has caused me this pain?" Your guidance might have important information for you about a person or about a current or past event.

_____

_____

_____

_____

_____

Dialogue About Passion, Purpose, and Joy

Sometimes our guidance has great ideas for us!

Ask your Divine guidance, "What do you want to tell me about my passion and purpose or about what my inner child needs to feel joyful?"

_____

_____

_____

_____

Once you feel clear regarding the truth and the loving actions, move on to step 5.

Step 5

Take the loving actions identified in step 4.

> **The loving actions I'm going to take are:**
>
> _____
>
> _____
>
> _____
>
> _____
>
> _____

   Once you take the loving action, or at least imagine taking it, if you can't immediately take it, move on to step 6.

Step 6

Evaluate the action or actions by checking in with how you feel as a result.

> **The loving adult asks the inner child, "What are you feeling and experiencing as a result of the loving action or actions I took or plan to take as soon as I can?"**
>
> _____
>
> _____
>
> _____
>
> _____

   If you are not feeling better, go back to step 4 and ask your Divine guidance for another loving action.

Inner Bonding Is a Way of Living

Turning this practice into a daily way of life is what will protect you from going back into the behaviors and patterns from the past. With practice, you learn to keep a loving relationship with yourself throughout your life, no matter the challenges that come at you. This loving relationship between yourself and your Divine guidance fills you and empowers you to handle life's challenges with strength and equanimity.

Our brains are capable of creating new, healthy habits. The more you practice Inner Bonding, the more you will be creating and operating from the new neural pathways in your higher brain rather than from your old beliefs and behaviors lodged in your lower brain.

Inner Bonding is inclusive of all other healing paths, and there are many other modalities that can support your Inner Bonding practice. Psychotherapy, spiritual practices, body therapies, and trauma therapies can be supportive on your healing journey. Just be sure to ask your guidance, "Is this loving to me? Is this in my highest good?" rather than allowing external experts and authorities tell you what they believe you should be doing. Through the practice of Inner Bonding, you become your own best resource!

You might want to copy this list and have it with you to remind you of the steps until they become natural to you.

The Six Steps of Inner Bonding

Step 1: Be Willing to Feel Pain and Take Responsibility for Your Feelings

Step 2: Move into the Intent to Learn

Step 3: Dialogue with Your Inner Child and Your Wounded Self

Step 4: Dialogue with Your Divine Guidance

Step 5: Take Loving Action

Step 6: Evaluate Your Actions

Conclusion

How Divine Connection and Loving Ourselves Can Benefit Our Planet

Have you heard of the butterfly effect? The theory states that when a butterfly moves its wings at just the right time in one part of the world, that movement can, at some point in the future, cause a hurricane in another part of the world. The concept is that small changes, under certain conditions, can set off a series of effects that can ultimately lead to a massive impact, positive or negative, somewhere on our planet. I love this idea. How might your life change if you knew that your loving or unloving thoughts and actions toward yourself and others may have a significant impact on our world?

By learning to operate as a loving adult in connection with your Divine guidance, you could have a profound positive effect on our planet. Imagine the kind of world we would have if everyone was devoted to taking responsibility for their feelings and learned to love themselves and others. If a butterfly's wings can cause a hurricane, imagine what we can create by learning to love ourselves.

There is another interesting theory called the "Hundredth Monkey," which was described by Ken Keyes Jr. In the 1950s, scientists gave dirty sweet potatoes to monkeys living on an island. The monkeys liked the potatoes, but they didn't like the dirt. Some monkeys learned to wash their potatoes, and eventually most of the monkeys on the island were washing their dirty potatoes. Then an amazing thing happened. Monkeys on a different island, some distance away from the first, who had also been given dirty potatoes, spontaneously started to wash their potatoes as well! The Hundredth Monkey theory states that when enough people are doing something, spontaneously many others will also start to do it.

I believe that when enough of us are loving ourselves, taking responsibility for our feelings and sharing our love, wonderful things will occur. Here is what I imagine and hope will happen.

Kindness Becomes a Way of Life

As you deepen your Inner Bonding practice, you will notice that the kinder you are to yourself, the more you find yourself feeling kindly toward others. Have you noticed how often videos of individual kind acts go viral on social media? I love that they do go viral, but I'm also sad that kindness is so unusual that it needs to be filmed and put on YouTube. If people learned to be kind to themselves, they would naturally be kind to each other.

The more you see and value your own beautiful soul essence, the easier it is to see and value the essence of others. The more you define yourself by your wonderful intrinsic qualities, the more you are able to see past the external qualities of others and into who they really are.

Imagine how life would be if we related to ourselves and to each other as our soul essences, rather than making judgments based on looks, performance, status, money, skin color, ethnicity, nationality, gender, or sexual orientation. Imagine what child-rearing and education would be like if parents could see, value, and mirror the essence of their children, and teachers appreciated their students' essence rather than ever judging them by their performance.

We Are No Longer Controlled by Others

When you are not connected with your feelings—your inner guidance—and you are not connected with your Divine guidance, you can be easily manipulated by others and by the media. We know truth by what we feel and by accessing our Divine guidance. When we are emotionally shut down or numbed by medication or recreational drugs or by sugar and processed foods, our frequency is too low to access our guidance, and we have no way of knowing what's true.

Imagine being able to discern the truth. It's easy to stay with your own inner knowing when you are connected with your feelings and your Divine guidance. When your frequency is high, because you love yourself enough to move beyond junk foods and junk thoughts, you will be surprised by how quickly you can distinguish the truth from the lies. This inner knowing provides us with great freedom to make choices based on what's in our highest good rather than on what some authority tells us is right for us.

Major Social and Economic Issues Are Resolved

We can't solve the problems on our planet if we are acting from our wounded selves, because all the issues we face result from the fear and greed of the wounded self. Trying to solve the problems externally will never lead to inner or planetary peace.

Sometimes we wonder how people can live with themselves when they are causing harm. The answer is that people who cause harm are disconnected from their soul and their Divine guidance and are being ruled by their wounded self. When money and power over others becomes more important than love and caring, we find ourselves in big trouble. I am heartbroken over how many people get both physically and emotionally sick or are dying from the junk that passes as food in our grocery stores and from the drugs they take to dull their physical and emotional pain. It all comes from the wounded self's greed and desire for power over others. I often wonder what it will take for people to realize that we are here on the planet to evolve in love and to manifest love. This is summed up in a quote by Jimi Hendrix: "When the power of love overcomes the love of power, the world will know peace."

For things to change, it's going to take the people of our beautiful planet getting smarter and taking courageous steps. We are not helpless to bring about change. We can all take the first steps by first learning to love ourselves through our Inner Bonding practice and then modeling our love to others. Love heals, and as more of us come from love, the faster this much-needed healing will occur. Imagine how easy it would be to resolve all the social and economic issues plaguing our planet if each of us were taking responsibility for our feelings and filling ourselves up with love, so that we didn't need to fill up with money and things. Imagine how easy it would be to resolve our current pressing issues if love were our guiding light.

Knowing We Are One

As we embrace the beauty of our own essence, we are naturally able to see the essence of others, and that's when we have the experience of knowing that we are all one. Years ago, my guidance gave me an image that I've found helpful. She told me to picture all living beings as the pieces of a giant puzzle. Each piece has a different shape and color, but none is more important than any other. If one piece is missing, whether it's on the edge or in the middle, the puzzle isn't complete; only all together do they form a whole. She said that each of us is a piece in that puzzle and the whole of the puzzle is Spirit. Each piece has its special job in the whole of the puzzle. Together, we are one. She told me that the energy of Divine Love isn't static—it's a continuously evolving energy, and that as each of us evolves in our ability to love, the energy of love evolves. Each of us is vitally important to this process.

If each person on the planet knew that we are all one, we would not be able to hurt each other. Just as we know that harming some of the cells in our body affects our whole body, harming one of us affects all of us. If we knew we are one, all of the problems that currently plague us would resolve. There would be no "us" and "them." There would just be us—all of us together—sharing love on our beautiful planet and supporting ourselves and each other in our highest good.

These are my dreams, my visions, for how Inner Bonding can benefit the whole. So as you complete this workbook and bring its processes into your life, know that the best thing you can do for yourself and for our planet is to be guided by your Divine guidance to learn to love yourself and share your love with others.

Acknowledgments

I am deeply grateful to Wendy Millstine, acquisitions editor at New Harbinger, for recognizing the value of Inner Bonding and reaching out to me to write this workbook. Working with the staff of New Harbinger has been a joy. Jennye Garibaldi, Jennifer Holder, and Jennifer Eastman have been amazing editors, and Vicraj Gill has graciously helped me learn how to set up a small recording studio in my home to record the visualizations. New Harbinger rocks!

I am so grateful for Dr. Erika Chopich. She is the only person who can accurately assess my writing, because she is not only the most brilliant, creative, funniest, playful, generous, and caring person I know but she is also the co-creator of Inner Bonding. She is my closest friend, the person I laugh with the most, and the person I go to for help with any challenge I have. She is my "Golden Girl" housemate, with whom I am never lonely.

I am deeply grateful for my Inner Bonding team, without whom I would have no time to write. They have been with me for many years, and I love them dearly. Deep thanks to Valerie Lippincott, our wonderful assistant; Guy Ewing, our incredible webmaster; Karen Kral, the creator of our Inner Bonding Facilitator Training Program (IBFTP) and codirector of training; and Stel Fine, director of expansion and codirector of training.

Finally, I am profoundly grateful for my Divine guidance, who never leaves me alone, who is always guiding me, moment by moment, and whom I can always turn to for wisdom, love, compassion, and comfort. She is a constant presence in my life, and I would not know how to navigate my life without her.

Resources

Inner Bonding Resources

Companion book: *Diet for Divine Connection: Beyond Junk Foods and Junk Thoughts to At-Will Spiritual Connection* (Light Technology Publishing, 2018).

For information or to schedule a phone or Skype session: call 310–459–1700 or 888–646–6372 (888–6INNERBOND).

Internet Resources

Inner Bonding—The Power To Heal Yourself! https://www.innerbonding.com

Free Inner Bonding course, https://www.innerbonding.com/welcome

Thirty-day at-home Inner Bonding courses: "Love Yourself," "Frequency," "Attracting Your Beloved," and "Passionate Purpose, Vibrant Health" at https://www.innerbonding.com/show-page/159/home-study-courses.html

SelfQuest—the Inner Bonding online program—teaches Inner Bonding in an in-depth way online: http://selfquest.com

Inner Bonding Facilitator Training Program, to become a certified Inner Bonding facilitator: https://www.innerbonding.com/show-page/339/ibftp.html

Books, lectures, workshops, podcasts, webinars, and e-books: https://www.innerbonding.com/store.php

Events, workshops, intensives, and support groups: https://www.innerbonding.com/events.php

Health Resources

More on the Gut-Brain Connection

Natasha Campbell-McBride, MD, *The Gut and Psychology Syndrome* (Medinform Publishing, 2010).

David Perlmutter, MD, *Grain Brain* (New York: Little, Brown, 2013) and *Brain Maker* (New York: Little, Brown, 2015).

The Cookbooks I Use A Lot

Sally Fallon, *Nourishing Traditions: The Cookbook That Challenges Politically Correct Nutrition and Diet Dictocrats* (Washington, DC: NewTrends, 2001).

Wardeh Harmon, *The Complete Idiot's Guide to Fermenting Foods* (New York: Penguin, 2012).

My Favorite Food Websites

Organic sprouted flour and grains: https://healthyflour.com

Traditional cultures for yogurt, cheese, and sourdough bread, with excellent videos: https://www.culturesforhealth.com

Whole food organic supplements: https://www.thesynergycompany.com

My Favorite Health Information Websites

Mercola: Take Total Control of Your Health (the website of Dr. Joseph Mercola): https://www.mercola.com

MindBodyGreen: https://www.mindbodygreen.com

Margaret Paul, PhD, is cocreator of the powerful Inner Bonding® self-healing process and the related SelfQuest® self-healing software program. Paul holds a PhD in psychology, has appeared on numerous radio and television shows, and has been counseling individuals and couples since 1968. She has led groups, taught classes and workshops, and worked with partnerships and businesses since 1973, and has been speaking publicly and teaching Inner Bonding seminars and workshops since 1983—both nationally and internationally. Paul is on the faculty at The Shift Network, has taught at the Kripalu Center for many years, and is also currently teaching at The Art of Living Center and 1440 Multiversity. She is coauthor of *Do I Have to Give Up Me to Be Loved By You?*, *Do I Have to Give Up Me to Be Loved By My Kids?*, *Do I Have to Give Up Me to Be Loved By You Workbook*, *Healing Your Aloneness*, and *The Healing Your Aloneness Workbook*; and author of *Inner Bonding*, *Do I Have to Give Up Me to Be Loved By God?*, and *Diet for Divine Connection*. Her books have been translated into eleven languages.

Foreword writer **Katherine Woodward Thomas** is author of the *New York Times* bestsellers *Calling in "The One"* and *Conscious Uncoupling*, which inspired the conscious divorce of actress Gwyneth Paltrow and musician Chris Martin, and launched a movement towards kinder, more respectful breakups and divorce. Katherine is a licensed marriage and family therapist, and teacher to hundreds of thousands of people from all around the world in her virtual and in-person learning communities.

For more information, please visit www.katherinewoodwardthomas.com.

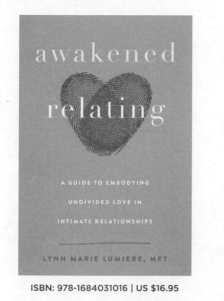

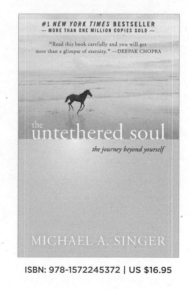

Real change *is* possible

For more than forty-five years, New Harbinger has published proven-effective self-help books and pioneering workbooks to help readers of all ages and backgrounds improve mental health and well-being, and achieve lasting personal growth. In addition, our spirituality books offer profound guidance for deepening awareness and cultivating healing, self-discovery, and fulfillment.

Founded by psychologist Matthew McKay and Patrick Fanning, New Harbinger is proud to be an independent, employee-owned company. Our books reflect our core values of integrity, innovation, commitment, sustainability, compassion, and trust. Written by leaders in the field and recommended by therapists worldwide, New Harbinger books are practical, accessible, and provide real tools for real change.

Register your **new harbinger** titles for additional benefits!

When you register your **new harbinger** title—purchased in any format, from any source—you get access to benefits like the following:

- Downloadable accessories like printable worksheets and extra content

- Instructional videos and audio files

- Information about updates, corrections, and new editions

Not every title has accessories, but we're adding new material all the time.

Access free accessories in 3 easy steps:

1. Sign in at NewHarbinger.com (or **register** to create an account).

2. Click on **register a book**. Search for your title and click the **register** button when it appears.

3. Click on the **book cover or title** to go to its details page. Click on **accessories** to view and access files.

That's all there is to it!

If you need help, visit:

NewHarbinger.com/accessories